WHAT IS THIS TREASURE

By the Same Author

A TIME FOR CHRISTIAN CANDOR

DOING THE TRUTH

TEEN-AGERS AND SEX

IF YOU MARRY OUTSIDE YOUR FAITH

BEYOND ANXIETY

THE NEXT DAY

A NEW LOOK IN PREACHING

BEYOND THE LAW

A CHRISTMAS CHALLENGE

CASES AND OTHER MATERIALS ON THE
    NEW FEDERAL AND CODE PROCEDURE

ADMINISTRATIVE LAW
    with Henry G. Fischer

THE FAITH OF THE CHURCH
    with W. Norman Pittenger

ROADBLOCKS TO FAITH
    with John McG. Krumm

THE CHURCH, POLITICS AND SOCIETY
    with John W. Pyle

MAN IN THE MIDDLE
    with Howard A. Johnson

JAMES A. PIKE

What is This Treasure

But we have this treasure in earthen vessels,
that the excellency of the power may be of God,
and not of us.

—II CORINTHIANS 4:7, AV

Harper & Row, Publishers

NEW YORK

Unless otherwise indicated, quotations from the Old Testament and from the Apocrypha are from the Revised Standard Version; those from the New Testament are from *The New English Bible*.

FIRST EDITION

LIBRARY OF CONGRESS CATALOG CARD NUMBER: 66-11484

B-Q

TO

PAUL TILLICH

PRINCIPAL MENTOR AND
DEAR FRIEND MUCH MISSED

AND

✠ JOHN A. T. ROBINSON

GOOD FRIEND AND
COMPANION-SPIRIT ALONG
THE WAY

Contents

Why This Book?

In the religious spectrum ranging from atheism to orthodoxy there is one category most neglected by preachers and writers: people who are conscious of believing in some things but who think they don't believe enough. Some with this self-estimate, while not bolting from the denomination in which they were brought up, nevertheless feel hypocritical and tend to display their halfway position by attending Church less and less frequently. Other such drop the Church in genuine sincerity—generally without animosity, perhaps even with a wish that they could "buy the whole package," and almost always with a trace of nostalgia.

It is to these people that this book is primarily addressed. But immediately I want to say—before those who think they are secularists or those who think they are orthodox believers stop reading this book—that through my talking to those in the in-between group, those of the rejecting "left" and of the religious "right" may perchance hear something which may challenge convictions heretofore insufficiently reflected upon. As to those in these two categories who are willing to continue to read, I will be frank as to my hopes.

As to the "unbeliever," I hope that this attempt at restatement of the Christian faith will suggest that it has a measure of credibility after all.

As to the "orthodox," I hope that it may bring what is "the heart of the matter" into bolder relief, opening the possibility of deeper faith and action more consistent therewith. I hope too that they may come to center on the few essentials and minimize the nonessentials, with the result that there may be a greater readiness to become bedfellows with the less "orthodox" and that they will constitute less of a barrier to belief on the part of those outside.

This last suggests another aim of the author. As many of my readers may well know, I have a passion for church unity—to the point of having been called an "ecumaniac." Perhaps the most important block in the mind of church people at the grass roots is the assumption that there are important differences between the respective church bodies. Differences there are. But essential differences? Perhaps not. And the only way we can know the answer is to seek to distinguish what is essential and what is nonessential (though perhaps desirable).

The "orthodox" and the "denominational guardians," threatened by any attempt at a redo of theology, have a denigrating word for it: *reductionism.** Sometimes the handiest name for a movement is supplied by its enemies. The Wesleyans were labeled "methodists" by hostile members of our Church. Members of the Society of Friends were similarly denominated "quakers." And two of the most convenient (albeit somewhat misleading) names for the Christian movement for an existentialist and relativistic ethic were supplied by the Papacy—"The New Morality" and "situational ethics."

I cannot speak for my fellow spirits in the current theological revolution; but personally I gladly accept the label "reductionism" as representing a good half-truth. The enterprise of which this book is an example is, hopefully, not reductive as to the quality and depth of faith and commitment and as to the breadth of action springing therefrom. But it is reductive as to the number of *items* regarded as essential to authentic Christianity.

Now the reductive process in any field of thought is bound to

* E.g., Mascall, *The Secularisation of Christianity* (London: Darton, Longman & Todd Ltd., 1965), *passim.*

be iconoclastic as well as constructive. And since any thinker and writer is finite, one does not always succeed in performing both tasks at once or keeping the results in balance in any one address, essay, or book. I owe it to the insight of the publishers (more especially of Mr. Eugene Exman, recently retired, and Mr. Melvin Arnold) that I undertook this work as a needed sequel to *A Time for Christian Candor,* published in the fall of 1964. That book was predominantly iconoclastic, citing chapter and verse across the whole range of doctrine, ethics, and cultic practice. True, its latter chapters were an attempt to put Humpty Dumpty back together again—but fairly unsystematically; and on some points its positive assertions were somewhat unconvincing—not only to readers but in some instances to the author (I did read the book after it came out). In the light of this self-estimate I am of course grateful to many people who affirmed that through the book they gained a new hold on their faith and to those who said that because of reading it they had come into the Church. But I am even more grateful to my critics (and they were many—in fact too many to credit by name), particularly those who shared my conviction as to the necessity for this task in our times but who perceptively put the finger on one or another weak link in the chain. It is due to their help, many conversations with individuals—"orthodox," secularist, and in the grayer area in between—and considerable further reflection that the pages which follow present more coherently what I believe the basic Catholic Faith to be. I have had further thoughts as to what is *not;* and this is developed on some points more fully than in *Christian Candor,* but those who want the negative spelled out more extensively I refer to the earlier volume.

There have been other helpers along the way whom it is a joy to acknowledge: my wife and immediate colleagues with whom there has been much dialogue on these matters—my episcopal brother, the Rt. Rev. G. Richard Millard, s.t.m., d.d.; the

Rev. David Baar, my Chaplain; the Rev. Spencer Rice, of the Diocesan staff; the Rev. Canon Robert W. Cromey; and Col. Howard Freeman, of the Diocesan staff. For the careful typing and checking the manuscript I wish to acknowledge Miss Myrtle Goodwin, my secretary, Mrs. Binnie Graham and Mrs. Gladys Allen, of the secretarial staff. Very stimulating to my thinking were the attendants at the Aspen Institute for Humanistic Studies, July 15—30, 1965, especially Mr. Maco Stewart; those participating in the Family Conference of the Fremont Presbyterian Church of Sacramento, at Lake Tahoe the first week in September, especially the Rev. Robert R. Ferguson, D.D., the Senior Minister, Mrs. Ferguson, who spent many hours in assistance in the preparation of the manuscript, Miss Anne Fricker, who was kind enough to check Biblical quotations and references, and Dr. and Mrs. Thomas Harris; Dr. Alan Watts and the others at the seminar on this subject at the Esalen Institute at Big Sur, last fall; Mr. Roy Franklin Steward, of Meriden, Connecticut, an especially interested layman; and the clergy and people of Trinity Church, New York City (and especially my dear friend the Rector, the Rev. John Heuss, D.D.), where, serving as Select Preacher in the Summer of 1964, I began the articulation of some of the approaches reflected in these pages.

Fruitful too were conversations with my episcopal brethren at the meeting of the House of Bishops at Glacier Park in September, at which was rejected the petition of thirteen Arizona priests, supported by "Concerned Episcopalians" of Selma, Alabama, that I be declared a heretic, asked to recant, or be tried and deposed.

I wish to call special attention to the statement unanimously approved by the House*—not as furnishing an *imprimatur* (our

---

* Presented by the House's Committee on Theology, consisting of the Rt. Rev. Richard S. M. Emrich, PH.D. (chairman), the Rt. Rev. Stephen F. Bayne, S.T.D., the Rt. Rev. Jonathan M. Sherman, S.T.D., the Rt. Rev. Walter C. Klein, PH.D., the Rt. Rev. William F. Creighton, D.D. (substituting for the Rt. Rev. Angus Dun, S.T.D.), and the author (who for obvious reasons was disqualified from serving on this particular occasion).

Church requires none) for this book, but as providing what can be thought of as a Charter for the current movement among Anglicans, variously called "the Theological Revolution," "the Second Reformation," "the Cambridge-Southwark Axis" (a label liked neither at Cambridge nor in the Diocese of Southwark. To my knowledge this is the first official ecclesiastical declaration as to the nature and value of theological reconstruction and the role of the Church and of the individual in its pursuit. After those sentences "clearing" the present author, the statement reads:

Nor will we limit the historic disciplined liberty of the theological inquiry and the necessary devout testing of the vessels of Christian belief. Language changes; the concepts which are the furniture of men's minds change; the Faith given in the mighty acts of God does not change. Nor do we doubt that many an allegation of heterodoxy against any of us, or our clergy, is in fact a covert attack on legitimate Christian social concern and action.

It is a good thing responsibly to explore alternative ways of stating our unchanging Faith and to press for amendments in Church order. We are indebted to many for such pioneering exploration. Continuity and change are both facts of life to be held in fruitful tension.

Because of misunderstandings which so easily occur, we say to those outside and inside the Church that the Church's Faith is expressed in its title deeds—the Scriptures, and the Creeds which guard them— and in the prayers and sacramental acts in the Book of Common Prayer which express Christ's continuing ministry within the Church. Let no publicity mislead anyone as to the sincerity with which this Church and its people accept the historic Christian Faith and try to live it. An individual may well claim the freedom to think aloud, to discuss, to explore. But when he does, whatever his station, he does so as one member of Christ's Body. Only the whole Body, speaking maturely and corporately, can officially define the Faith it confesses before its Lord. Individual speculations or opinions are just that.

The stake of the whole Church in the task of such individual efforts is underlined by the comment to the press, after the

House's adoption of the statement, by the Rt. Rev. John E. Hines, D.D., Presiding Bishop of the Episcopal Church: "As you can see by today's action, the House of Bishops undertakes to support their bishops in battling for the truth. The Episcopal Church will continue to go forward in its exploring of ways and means of making the Gospel understandable to the contemporary world. We may often be misunderstood and attacked by old school, conservative thinkers, but the Church will not retreat."

"Making the Gospel understandable" is the aim of this effort. At the risk of facing a review which begins "This thin volume . . ." (with a likely double entendre in the use of the adjective!), I have here made an earnest try to write simply, not because I am in advance adjudging the readers to be simple-minded, but because all of us—"professionals" and interested amateurs alike— have been plagued with the question, "If it is all that true, and if it is catholic, why does it sound so complicated?" Complexity and esotericity (unintentionally quasi-gnostic), on the one hand, and superficiality and obviousity, on the other, are the Scylla and Charybdis of the modern theological enterprise. The degree to which this effort escapes the rock and the whirlpool the reviewers and readers can judge. But a course between has been the aim.

✠ JAMES A. PIKE

Nazareth, Israel
Christmas Eve, 1965

WHAT IS THIS TREASURE

I

All That

Not long ago a thoughtful young lady said to me, "I've always rather liked to go to Church, but I don't go much anymore because I must confess I don't really believe all that." I had no reason to believe that this was a rationalization intended to cover the fact that she preferred to sleep in and/or browse over the Sunday paper Sunday mornings, or that she had been "brushed" by the lady pillars of the parish, or that she had been disillusioned by the character—or put off by the personality—of the pastor. She said what she meant, and she meant what she said. More than that, her saying it reflected something commendable. It would be good if more churchmen were thinking enough about religion that such an admission would be possible.

There are two possible responses to such a statement, taken at face value: one, an approach to the heart and will, centering on the words "don't really believe"; the other, an approach to the mind, centering on the words "all that." I chose the latter course. Sound as basic Christianity is, those pastors or evangelists who plead "Just believe!"—though correct in their premise that an act of faith is in any case essential—overlook the fact the precisely the same appeal could be made by a devotee of astrology or of Rosicrucianism, or by one who centers his devotional life on "the Black Mass." Often such well-intentioned apostles are really saying "Have faith in faith."

So I started with "What do you mean by 'all that'?" Acquainted from childhood with the complex lore of the Church, she rattled off a long list of propositions which could be grouped under the three C's of religion: Creed, Code, and Cult. To these my response was varied: "I don't believe that myself." "That's not essential." "I'm an agnostic on that point." "That commandment isn't binding: sometimes it would represent the thing to do, sometimes not." "That's just a custom—and not a very ancient one at that; God didn't prescribe it." "That doctrine stands for something true; but the conventional way of putting it doesn't speak to me either."

This brought the response, "Well, what is a person supposed to be able to believe and belong in the Church?" Which is another way of asking, "What is *all that?*" This was an invitation to deliver a speech. But dialogue is more in fashion today; so, instead I said, "Let's see what you do believe."

"Do you believe in a universe?" I began. "That is, do you believe that everything is sort of all tied together?" She nodded her head.

"Though the universe consists of billions and billions of separate things, do you believe that in and under and through all of it there is one unifying reality?"

"Yes, that makes sense. I gather that you mean 'God.'"

"Sure," I replied. "But that doesn't get us very far without the next question: Do you think that His nature and qualities would be less than—or at least equal to or more than—the most highly developed being evolved, that is, people like us?"

"Well, put that way," she replied, "I would say the latter. He'd have at least all we've got."

"And we've got a lot," I continued. "We sort of take it for granted; but a man can tie together past, present, and future; he can love and be loved; he is conscious of his experience and of himself; he can relate to other persons with his strength and inspiration; he can reveal his knowledge and—to a degree—his inner self to others, if they are really open to him, that is, he can be articulate—"

"—and so it would be reasonable to suppose," she carried on, "that God is like that."

"And more. But as I suggested, I can only reveal myself to someone else to the degree that he is really 'open' to me. He may appear to be in conversation, but if he's preoccupied with himself or some specific concern, he really won't get very fully what I'm trying to say—or mean. He really won't get to know me."

"With all due respect to you," she interrupted, "what's that got to do with religion or God?"

"A lot," I went on. "From what you know about Jesus as seen in the New Testament, wouldn't you say that He seemed to have no preoccupation with Himself, didn't worry about what people thought about Him, was so committed to His mission of serving others that He was the fully 'open' man—and so there were no barriers to God's revealing Himself to Him and through Him to others around Him?"

"Yes, that hangs together. It reminds me of a text beginning 'God was in Christ . . .'"

"Right." I continued, "'. . . reconciling the world to Himself' (2 Cor. 5:19). And St. Paul put it another way: '. . . in him dwelleth all the fulness of the Godhead bodily . . .' (Col. 2:9)!"

"That's fine," she agreed, "but what's that got to do with me?"

"Everything," I asserted. "Jesus was in every sense a human being just as we are. Like us He was free to make decisions, including the big decision of what He would do with His life. He freely chose to do what He believed God wanted Him to do. He didn't care whether He 'fit in' or 'got ahead.' And He didn't. He not only taught in one-hundred-per-cent terms the full dimension of human freedom from the idols (and they were the same ones that cramp people today from true freedom, self-fulfillment, and loving service to others), but He fully lived it. So not only His words but His very being were a standing threat to different types around Him, and they vented their hostilities toward Him, ganged up on Him and had Him convicted and executed."

"Being the best, He suffered the worst," she concluded.

"I can see that you feel sympathy; but more than that is involved. You can identify with Him in the worst that has ever happened to you—or can happen."

"But what good does that do?" she asked quite reasonably.

"Not much, if it weren't for one thing. Can you believe that each human being is so special, so unique, so precious that he goes on as a person forever?"

"Put that way," she answered, "that seems more likely than not."

"Well, does it seem surprising to you that since Jesus was so transparent in character, the ever available power of God could so fully show through Him that the ongoingness of His personality was vividly sensed by those who were closest to Him and who had become very 'open' to Him?"

"That seems plausible. I remember that they had their troubles, too, when they began to go around saying that Jesus lived, when his enemies thought they had gotten rid of Him."

"Very much so. But they were courageous and joyous too, because in this they not only identified with His sufferings and Cross but also with His ongoing life, victorious over anything men could do."

She picked it up from here. "I can see that would be attractive to people—especially to those groping for a meaning for life and wanting to be courageous and confident. I guess that's why the whole thing spread so fast. But with weeks, years, and decades going by, you'd think that all this would have grown dimmer and dimmer, and that in fact people in later centuries would have practically nothing left from it to hold on to—or, as you put it, to identify with."

"It would have—and soon," I readily conceded, "were it not

for three things: first, they were very eager to tell other people about it—and thus kept reinforcing it in themselves; second, using a Jewish ceremony familiar at the time—baptism—they dramatically initiated each new believer into their community, acting out Death and Resurrection; and third, also following a familiar Jewish usage of sharing in bread and wine, they 'celebrated' all this through the remembering of His death and Resurrection—and so kept reidentifying. The reality of this constantly renewing experience was well expressed by St. Luke: 'He was known of them in the breaking of the bread' (24:35). And so it has been for about two thousand years now. For those who keep on using these ways of remembering, the past is always present—and future. It's eternal—though grounded in time and history.'"

"And as for those who stop going to Church—" she interrupted.

"It *does* grow dimmer."

"I can see that," she granted. "Why can't I work at keeping this alive alone without getting involved in the Church?'"

"You can—and should. But faith begets faith—it's contagious. We are by nature social beings and one way God breaks through is in what we call 'esprit de corps'—His Holy Spirit."

"But," she queried, "you used the phrase 'breaks through' once before and then you were talking about His getting through because of the 'openness' of Jesus."

"Right," I answered. "But you'll notice that God was the subject of the sentence in each case. He who is unchanging and ever available is the Source and Revealer throughout. We keep identifying with God in Christ through His Spirit *now;* and as we can thereby become more and more open ourselves, His power and love and new life more and more can 'break through' to us and through us to others."

"And?"

"That's all there is to it. I don't quite mean that. There have

been lots of ways of saying it—and acting it out. But in terms of essentials, that's all. Which reminds me of the 'all that' which closed your candid declaration 'I don't really believe all that.' "

"That's all . . . all that," she ruminated. "These sound about the same; if they really are, then I'm *with* it."

"I'm glad we talked," I said. "It would seem that the outcome could be *fewer beliefs, more belief.*"

2

Revealing Images of God

THERE WAS A MAN a long time ago who believed that only God is wise; and through dialogue with others in his community he came to the conclusion that his own wisdom, above other men, consisted in the fact that he knew this and that apparently they did not. He sought through conversation to assert this priority of God as over both "the gods" and human pretensions.

His contemporaries found this threatening; and brought him to trial for nonconformity with the established religion. Fortunately we have a relatively faithful account of his reactions during the trial and up to the time of his execution, and thus are afforded a window into the center of this man's being and an avenue to the central convictions which undergirded the consistency of his behavior in the time of his testing.

The character revealed? Unflinching courage, no fear of death; no care for material things or reputation; love and respect for the State, and forgiveness of his persecutors but unwillingness to compromise his higher loyalty to truth; and confidence in the value of his witness and the future of his cause; consistency of teaching and action.

Out of what convictions? One God, a man's responsibility to serve Him in this life in the way he feels called, and confidence that beyond death is good—indeed, that in the ultimate sense no evil can happen to a good man.

Some of the words attributed to him which most reveal him:

"And so leaving the event with God, in obedience to the law I will now make my defence."

"Then I went to one man after another, being not unconscious of the enmity which I provoked, and I lamented and feared this: But necessity was laid upon me,—the word of God, I thought ought to be considered first."

"This inquisition has led to my having many enemies of the worst and most dangerous kind, and has given occasion also to many calumnies. And I am called wise, for my hearers always imagine that I myself possess the wisdom which I find wanting in others: but the truth is . . . that God only is wise. . . . The wisdom of men is worth little or nothing."

". . . My occupation quite absorbs me, and I have no time to give either to any public matter of interest or to any concern of my own, but I am in utter poverty. . . ."

". . . And then if somebody asks them, Why, what evil does he practice or teach? they do not know, and cannot tell; but in order that they may not appear to be at a loss, they repeat the ready-made charges which are used against all philosophers about teaching things up in the clouds and under the earth, and having no gods, and making the worse appear the better cause; for they do not like to confess that their pretence of knowledge has been detected—which is the truth; and as they are numerous and ambitious and energetic, and are drawn up in battle array and have persuasive tongues, they have filled your ears with their loud and inveterate calumnies."

"And this . . . is the truth and the whole truth; I have concealed nothing, I have dissembled nothing. And yet, I know that my plainness of speech makes them hate me, and what is their hatred but a proof that I am speaking the truth? Hence has arisen the prejudice against me; and this is the reason of it, as you will find out either in this or in any future enquiry."

"I know only too well how many are the enmities which I have incurred, and this is what will be my destruction if I am destroyed; . . . the envy and detraction of the world, which has been the death of many good men, and will probably be the death of many more; there is no danger of my being the last of them.

"Some one will say: And are you not ashamed . . . of a course of life which is likely to bring you to an untimely end? To him I may fairly answer: There you are mistaken: a man who is good for anything ought not to calculate the chance of living or dying; he ought only to consider whether in doing anything he is doing right or wrong—acting the part of a good man or of a bad."

"If you say to me . . . you shall be let off, but upon one condition, that you are not to enquire and speculate in this way any more, and that if you are caught doing so again you shall die;—if this was the condition on which you let me go, I should reply: . . . I honor and love you; but I shall obey God rather than you, and while I have life and strength I shall never cease from exhorting any one whom I meet and saying to him after my manner; You, my friend . . . are you not ashamed of heaping up the greatest amount of money and honor and reputation, and caring so little about wisdom and truth and the greatest improvement of the soul, which you never regard or heed at all?"

"For I do nothing but go about persuading you all, old and young alike, not to take thought for your persons or your properties, but first and chiefly to care about the greatest improvement of the soul. I tell you that virtue is not given by money, but that from virtue comes money and every other good of man, public as well as private."

". . . Either acquit me or not; but whichever you do, understand that I shall never alter my ways, not even if I have to die many times."

"I would have you know, that if you kill such an one as I am, you will injure yourselves more than you will injure me. Nothing will injure me . . . for a bad man is not permitted to injure a better than himself. . . . For the evil of doing as he is doing—the evil of unjustly taking away the life of another—is greater far."

"I . . . am a sort of gadfly, given to the state by God; and the state is a great and noble steed who is tardy in his motions owing to his very size, and requires to be stirred into life. I am that gadfly which God has attached to the state, and all day long and in all places am always fastening upon you, arousing and persuading and reproaching you."

"When I say that I am given to you by God, the proof of my mission is this:—if I had been like other men, I should not have neglected all my own concerns or patiently seen the neglect of them during all these years, and have been doing yours, coming to you individually like a father or elder brother, exhorting you to regard virtue; such conduct, I say, would be unlike human nature. If I had gained anything, or if my ex- hortations had been paid, there would have been some sense in my doing so; but now, as you will perceive, not even the im- pudence of my accusers dares to say that I have ever exacted or sought pay of any one; of that they have no witness. And I have a sufficient witness to the truth of what I say—my poverty."

". . . I showed, not in word only, but in deed, that if I may be allowed to use such an expression, I cared not a straw for death, and that my great and only care was lest I should do an un- righteous or unholy thing. For the strong arm of that oppressive power did not frighten me into doing wrong; . . ."

"And to you and to God I commit my cause, to be deter- minded by you as is best for you and me."

"The difficulty, my friends, is not to avoid death, but to avoid unrighteousness; for that runs faster than death. I . . . move slowly, and the slower runner has overtaken me, and my ac- cusers are keen and quick, and the faster runner, who is un- righteousness, has overtaken them. And now I depart hence condemned by you to suffer the penalty of death,—they too go their ways condemned by the truth to suffer the penalty of villainy and wrong; and I must abide by my award—let them abide by theirs."

"And I prophesy to you who are my murderers, that immediately after my departure punishment far heavier than you have inflicted on me will surely await you. Me you have killed because you wanted to escape the accuser, and not to give an account of your lives. But that will not be as you suppose: far otherwise. For I say that there will be more accusers of you than there are now. . . . If you think that by killing men you can prevent some one from censuring your evil lives, you are mistaken; that is not a way of escape which is either possible or honorable; the easiest and the noblest way is not to be disabling others, but to be improving yourselves. This is the prophecy which I utter before my departure to the judges who have condemned me."

"Wherefore, O judges, be of good cheer about death, and know of a certainty, that no evil can happen to a good man, either in life or after death. For which reason also I am not angry with my condemners, or with my accusers; they have done me no harm, although they did not mean to do me any good. . . ."

"In questions of just, fair and foul, good and evil . . . ought we to follow the opinion of the many and to fear them; or the opinion of the one man who has understanding? ought we not to fear and reverence him more than all the rest of the world: and if we desert him shall we not destroy and injure the principle in us which may be assumed to be improved by justice and deteriorated by injustice. . . ."

"Then we must do no wrong. . . . Nor when injured injure in return, as the many imagine; for we must injure no one at all. . . ."

"Then we ought not to retaliate or render evil for evil to any one, whatever evil we may have suffered from him."

"Think not of life and children first, and of justice afterwards, but of justice first, that you may be justified. . . ."

"Now you depart in innocence, a sufferer and not a doer of evil; a victim, not of the laws but of men."

"Leave me then . . . to fulfill the will of God, and to follow whither he leads."

"And when we are punished, whether by imprisonment or stripes, the punishment is to be endured in silence. . . ."

"Friends. . . . Stay then a little, for we may as well talk with one another while there is time."

These words which have been preserved unveil a person gifted with intelligence and consistency of thought and action, with transparency of character, courage, love, and indomitable trust in God. Any one of us would want to be a person like this. There have been published from time to time letters from fathers to sons seeking to express the hope of one generation for another; the words quoted above may well serve finely to convey such an image.

Who is this man? Jesus? No, though there are parallels in the latter's words for each of the quotations above. One of the Hebrew prophets? No. A Christian martyr? No. As many of my readers may have known all along, he is Socrates, who was tried and put to death by the Athenian State five centuries before Christ.* The fact that we see expressed and acted out in the life

---

* The quotations are from Plato's *Apology* and *Crito*. The following Socrates is reported to have said about the life to come: "Let us reflect in another way, and we shall see that there is great reason to hope that death is good: for one of two things, either death is a state of nothingness and utter unconsciousness, or, as men say, there is a change and migration of the soul from this world to another. Now if you suppose that there is no consciousness, but a sleep like the sleep of him who is undisturbed even by dreams, death will be an unspeakable gain. . . . But if death is the journey to another place, and there, as men say, all the dead abide, what good, all my friends and judges, can be greater than this? If indeed when the pilgrim arrives in the world below, he is delivered from the professors of justice in this world, and finds the true judges who are said to give judgment there . . . sons of God who were righteous in their own life, that pilgrimage will be worth making. What would not man

and death of a non-Christian significant elements of the Christian Faith is not a threat to that faith but rather an affirmation of it. In such an example—and there are others—is disclosed the universal validity of the Christian pattern of meaning and action.

Perhaps for our day this is a more convincing place to begin. For this truth there is claimed no "special revelation"; in this doing of the truth there is posited no "special Providence." Nor is the bearer of this Good set before us as the fruit of a special incarnation. Nor does this manifestation claim to have been presaged by prophets; nor is it offered as the fulfillment of the Divine choosing of a people; rather we see a good and faithful man in a crisis who displays the noblest in man, and through this learn of God, man, and eternal life.

We see much of this, too, in the figure of Buddha, even in spite of the accompaniment of Oriental rather than Occidental religious images. He freely laid aside rank, caste, and wealth to

---

give if he might converse with Orpheus and Musaeus and Hesiod and Homer. Nay, if this be true, let me die again and again. I, myself, too, shall have a wonderful interest in their meeting and conversing with Palamedes and Ajax the son of Telemon, and any other ancient hero who has suffered death through an unjust judgment; and there will be no small pleasure as I think in comparing my own sufferings with theirs. Above all, I shall then be able to continue my search into truth and the soul's knowledge; and in this world, so also in the next. . . . What would not a man give, O judges, to be able to examine the leader of the great Trojan expedition; or Odysseus or Sisyphus, or innumerable others, men and women too! In another world they don't put a man to death for asking questions: assuredly not. For besides being happier than we are, they will be immortal if what is said is true.

"Wherefore, O judges, be of good cheer about death, and know of a certainty, that no evil can happen to a good man, either in life or after death. He and his are not neglected by the Gods nor has my own approaching end happened by mere chance. But we see clearly that the time had arrived when it was better for me to die and be released from trouble . . . the hour of departure has arrived, and we go our ways—I to die, and you to live. Which is better God only knows."

The above quotations and those in the text are from *The Dialogues of Plato,* trans. and ed. by B. Jowett (Oxford University Press, 3d ed., 1892), Vol. II, pp. 109-135, 143-156.

lead a life which would bring meaning to him and others, and when his own perfection brought him to the edge of eternal fulfillment, he chose to tarry to seek to bring others along with him on the road to men's destiny.

A fruitful glimpse into the meaning of the life of man with God is also provided by the negative impact on his contemporaries of the person (or archetype) imaged in the second chapter of the apocryphal Wisdom of Solomon (2:1, 12–24):

For they reasoned unsoundly, saying to themselves, "Short and sorrowful is our life, and there is no remedy when a man comes to his end, and no one has been known to return from Hades.

"Let us lie in wait for the righteous man, because he is inconvenient to us and opposes our actions; he reproaches us for sins against the law, and accuses us of sins against our training. He professes to have knowledge of God, and calls himself a servant of the Lord. He became to us a reproof of our thoughts; the very sight of him is a burden to us, because his manner of life is unlike that of others, and his ways are strange. We are considered by him as something base, and he avoids our ways as unclean; he calls the last end of the righteous happy, and boasts that God is his father. Let us see if his words are true, and let us test what will happen at the end of his life; for if the righteous man is God's son, he will help him, and will deliver him from the hand of his adversaries. Let us test him with insult and torture, that we may find out how gentle he is, and make trial of his forbearance. Let us condemn him to a shameful death, for according to what he says, he will be protected."

Thus they reasoned, but they were led astray, for their wickedness blinded them, and they did not know the secret purposes of God, nor hope for the wages of holiness, nor discern the prize for blameless souls; for God created man for incorruption, and made him in the image of his own eternity, but through the devil's envy death entered the world, and those who belong to his party experience it.

It is not accident that the above passage is a designated lection in the Book of Common Prayer for the Liturgy for Good Friday. (But not unsuitable would be a selection of the above quotations from the *Apology,* words attributed to Socrates.) Of the same genre is the image of Jesus given us in another Holy Week lection (the Epistle for Palm Sunday in several traditions), particularly these words selected from the passage: "Christ Jesus made himself of no reputation and took upon him the form of a servant and humbled himself, became obedient unto death, even the death of the cross."

Obviously Christianity is centered on an image which has universal validity, not in terms of logical proof but in terms of intuitive response—actual and potential—of men of many backgrounds and cultures, of "all sorts and conditions," to portrayals of the best of manhood—this *best* not necessarily being more there, but being more *evident* in times of ultimate testing, especially when the character thus displayed is consistent with such men's prior declarations in their teaching of others. The universal validity of the image on which Christianity is centered enormously strengthens its plausibility and its commendability as a catholic faith, that is, for all men and for all times; but at the same time this same universality embodies a challenge to the uniqueness of Christianity—and indeed of its Central Figure. It is to this problem we will turn next.

3

Jesus a Way? The Only Way?

As to the place of Jesus Christ, at least five different views have emerged.

Minimal significance. At one end of the spectrum is a rejection of His significance. Some have gone so far as to assert that He never lived at all, that the saga centering on Him was contrived. Others, readily granting His existence, have asserted that we know virtually nothing of His life and teachings. Others have maintained that Paul invented Christianity—a religion alien to the straightforward Judaism of the martyr-rabbi of Nazareth. Some, positing the general accuracy of the Gospels in reporting the teaching of Jesus, regard it as an unsound variation from Judaism.

"A great teacher." A more numerous group, while not making negative assertions of this type, more or less "damn with faint praise." They have an affirmative regard for the teachings of Jesus and for Him as a person. They would say that He is definitely one of the great "teachers" in human history. No eternal significance is attached to His death, though the nobility of His courage and the tragedy of a miscarriage of justice is recognized—and is seen as a striking example of "man's inhumanity to man." The response to His teachings ranges from philosophical and ethical analyses of their import to sentimental acceptance of the least challenging of them (those reacting this way often refer to Him as "the Carpenter of Nazareth" or "the Master").

The only Saviour. At the other end of the spectrum is a view

which has received explicit expression throughout the history of
Christianity, namely, that belief in Jesus, as the one and only
Incarnation of God, is the only route to salvation. Those members of the human race who have been told about Him, who
have accepted Him as Divine and who have been baptized in the
name of the Trinity may be saved; no others may enter the
Kingdom of Heaven.

The Saviour + broader salvation. More generous is the view
next in from the right: Jesus is the one and only Incarnation of
God in all time, and thus He is *qualitatively* different from any
other human being; but God's revelation to man and man's
possibility of salvation is not as limited as in the fifth view. This
breadth has been conceived of in different ways. Even conservative Roman Catholic theologians have granted that persons not
belonging to the body of the "true Church" can belong to "the
soul" of the Church if they are in "invincible ignorance" of the
truth of its claims, on a basis of their good works in accordance
with the "natural law." Others would speak of "the secular
work of the Holy Spirit," enlightening men quite beyond the
borders of the Christian Church. Some would stress the general
role of the Logos—"made flesh" in Jesus but also the true light
which lighteth every man that cometh into the world (John
1:7, AV). (Nevertheless, Jesus is viewed as ontologically of a different order of reality than anyone else thus illumined.)

There is another possible view, which would seem to fall
midway in the spectrum. Before it is posed for consideration
and analysis it would be well for us to evaluate the other common views already described. The two which are held principally by non-Christians will be discussed briefly; the two, one or
the other of which are held by most Christians but which represent barriers to non-Christians, will be analyzed at more length.

Minimal significance. The writing off of Jesus as not having
existed at all or as being of little significance is contradicted
both by sound scholarship and by the very existence in the

world of the Christian Church in the past nineteen centuries. No recognized scholar—Christian, Jewish, or secularist—today denies the existence of Jesus. Most scholars would say that we know something of His life and teaching from what is recorded in the Synoptic Gospels. As for the invention of Christianity by Paul, those making this assertion are as naïve as Christian fundamentalists in assuming that Gospels were written earlier than St. Paul's first epistles. And the Gospels, which were compiled from a variety of sources, do not seem to have been particularly influenced by specially Pauline motifs.

"A great teacher." The view which estimates Jesus as a fine teacher among the fine teachers runs into at least two countervailing considerations:

1. Neither Jesus Himself nor His early followers who made Christianity possible thought of Him only as a teacher; in the New Testament books there is a consistently strong focus upon His being and doing; eternal significance is seen in the latter as well as in the former.

2. Viewing Jesus as a whole person, including what we know of His life as well as of His teaching, He is in fact in the West— even for people who do not consciously attribute to Him a unique status—generally the norm by which other figures are measured. For example, even a Unitarian who would say that St. Francis of Assisi was very Christlike would not be likely to say that Jesus was "very Franciscan." In fact for many, many who would deny that He is in any sense unique, Jesus is in net result ultimate in that He is not looked beyond and judged by some other person or norm.

The only Saviour. The view which asserts Jesus' uniqueness to the point of maintaining that He is the only avenue to God and to entry into His Kingdom, quite apart from what it is saying about the meaning of Jesus, presents a conviction as to the character of God which should evoke—as to such a god— the response of atheism. Taking this point alone, there are a number of reasons why billions of people have not been Christians. They may have been so unfortunate as to have lived before the Christian era. Though "A.D." they may never have heard of Jesus Christ or His Church. In many centuries of its life the Church was not particularly missionary-minded. Some portions of the Church, e.g., the Eastern Orthodox Communion, are not even missionary-minded today. In fact since the official establishment of the Church by Constantine, mission has never primarily absorbed the energies of the Church as a whole—a strange thing, in the light of the fact that most Christians in most centuries ostensibly have believed that salvation is only through Jesus Christ. And many to whom Christ has in fact been preached, may have been denied the opportunity of hearing Him preached well. Many others who may have heard Him preached well have met too many Christians, many who say "Lord, Lord," but whose lives and attitudes have not persuasively commended their Lord.

And quite apart from these obvious quantitative and qualitative limitations on the mission of Christ on this planet, the fact is that our Earth is but a tiny part of a vast universe. Astronomers have estimated that there are probably at least half a million planets around various stars in various galaxies, on which conditions are such that human life, rather as we know it, is possible. And the law of averages would further imply that on many, many such "earths" there is conscious, sentient life.

Now to assume that basic fulfillment is denied through no fault of their own to perhaps octillions of persons living in the various eras of history on this and other planets, who have not had an adequate opportunity to respond to a single Figure who has been heard of by only a relatively small proportion of people who have lived on this one small planet of a small star in a third-rate galaxy on the edge of a relatively modest cluster within the universe—to assume this is to worship something like a "tribal god." We have hitherto used this phrase, denigratingly, of a god which a specific ethnic group, e.g., the Canaanites or the early Jews, regarded as their very own possession, whose interests—whether in judgment of or grace toward men—was limited to an easily identifiable group. Later Judaism got somewhat beyond this concept—though remaining even to this day somewhat "hung up" on it; Christianity from the time of Paul onward got well beyond it—and actualized the new breadth—as far as the specific ethnic and racial distinctions go. But this commendable development at its best until the time of Copernicus (understandably, since few knew any better) had as its outside limit earthmen ("He hath made of one blood all the nations which dwell on the face of *the earth*"). But this breadth was accepted only as a potential arena for the salvation of men. Within the narrow limits of persons on this particular planet there has been imposed a still much narrower limit: salvation only for those earthmen who have accepted Jesus.

Before Copernicus, virtually everyone believed in a three-layer universe: a flat earth, hell below and heaven above, with the sun, moon, and stars as sort of Christmas-tree decorations hung there for us by a beneficent Deity who resided above it all. That theological speculation up to that point took account of no more is understandable. What is astonishing is the post-Copernican geocentric parochialism which with little challenge has dominated Christian belief even up to this day. Many, many who know better astronomically still theologically indulge in the premise that this earth is the center of the universe and that its populace is the primary concern of God. Now we are in a Space Age, with elaborate preparations and experiments moving toward "on-the-spot" investigation of other planets; and there are no limits, theoretically—and in the end, practically—to the extension of this exploration (whether by personal visitation or other means) to planets of other solar systems. The result is that millions of people are in their basic attitude toward the universe at least catching up with Copernicus. But, theologically speaking, few Christians have really abandoned the old pre-Copernican world view.

It would seem obvious that if there is a God at all, He is not all this insignificant, that is, "earth-bound." He is the Ultimate Ground of all being, of the whole universe, and of all other personal beings who dwell therein—or He is not at all. Though with our limited human minds we do not know—and never will know—the full dimension of God's justice and love, we do know by analogy that it must be at least as noble and far-reaching as human justice and love at its best. When seen in human beings, arbitrary partiality is adjudged evil, not good.

But since we actually know nothing yet about personal life on other planets, let us return to earth, and we will see that what is said above applies with equal force to that parochialism even narrower than geocentric which has been the dominant "line" of Christians throughout the centuries, namely, that they—or a portion of them—are to be saved and the rest of mankind lost. Behind this lies either the concept of God whose breadth is not adequate even to qualify as a geocentric deity *or* the concept of a God who is downright immoral. In fact if there were such a God, human beings of any degree of nobility of character who have thought through the concept of limited salvation would have the integrity to reject salvation proffered in these terms. More than that, they would feel called upon to propagandize against loyalty on the part of others to such a God. What respect, for example, would we have for a civil rights demonstrator who at the time of crisis of arrest would be willing to escape jailing and sentence through the "good offices" of a friend who could "fix it up" with the district attorney or the judge. The same integrity which was the source of his witness in the first place would inspire him to want to be treated as an equal with his fellow witnesses in the cause. Nor would a really sensitive sibling—circumstances being relatively equal—accept from his father's estate a markedly greater proportion than was to be received by his brothers and sisters. And part of Socrates' nobility is his refusal to accept deliverance from the death sentence —a prize not offered by the State to other prisoners in a similar situation—at the hands of the well-connected Crito.

Many thoughtful Christians, when actually confronted by the incredibility of the limited salvation theory, will say well-meaningly, "But the Church doesn't really teach that!" What the norms are by which to judge what the Church (or any denomination of it) teaches, is too complex a subject to take up here. But this much may be said: *the preponderant emphasis in the New Testament, the Church Fathers, the corporately accepted theologians, and the official Confessions of Faith and liturgies, throughout the almost two millenna of the Church's history, clearly has come down on the side of an exclusivist view of salvation.* And, further, it is just a plain fact that if one counted noses, by far most of the Christians throughout the nineteen hundred years of the Church's existence have believed precisely that.

A few examples are sufficient. *From the Bible:* "No one comes to the Father except by me" (John 14:6). "God loved the world so much that he gave his only Son, that everyone who had faith in him may not die but have eternal life" (John 3:16). "Everything is entrusted to me by my Father; and no one knows the Son but the Father, and no one knows the Father but the Son and those to whom the Son may choose to reveal him" (Matt. 11:27=Luke 10:22).

Official liturgical language (here as in the case of doctrinal assertions it is more becoming for an Episcopal author to use Anglican examples—but examples from the other traditions are no better or no worse): "None can enter into the Kingdom of God, except he be regenerate and born anew of Water and of the Holy Ghost" (Book of Common Prayer, p. 273); ". . . there is none other Name under heaven given to man, in whom, and through whom, thou mayest receive health and salvation, but only the Name of our Lord Jesus Christ" (p. 314).

Official doctrine: the Articles of Religion, Article XVIII: "OF OBTAINING ETERNAL SALVATION ONLY BY THE NAME OF CHRIST. They also are to be had accursed that presume to say, That every man shall be saved by the Law or Sect which he professeth, so that he be diligent to frame his life according to that Law, and the light of Nature. For Holy Scripture doth set out unto us only the Name of Jesus Christ, whereby men must be saved."

The alternatives for reaction are clear: either (a) the New Testament and the preponderance of teaching of the Church throughout the centuries is flatly wrong, or (b) that the god thus taught about either does not exist or is subhuman in morality—with the moral consequence that belief in him (or if perchance such a god does exist, *he*) is to be opposed. Presumably anyone confronted clearly with these alternatives would opt for the former rather than for the latter.

The Saviour+broader salvation. The intolerability of the approach just treated has been evident to critical Christian thinkers for a long time and thus there have emerged in various traditions ways of qualifying it—theories which have become official, semiofficial, or permissible in several Christian bodies. The principal approaches are the following:

1. *The general Logos.* One format for the doctrine of the Incarnation is that the articulating, implementing character within God, the Word, "became flesh; he came to dwell among us" (John 1:14). Such an approach leaves open the general work of the Logos—in creation and in the illumination of men's minds: "the true light, which lighteth every man that cometh into the world (John 1:9, AV). Apart from the dubiety of this and other translations which seem to give some "breathing room" of generous proportions, it does afford a basis for the important affirmation that all truth is God's truth wherever and however it is manifested. Nevertheless, it is clear from the immediate context that the evangelist does not offer it as an avenue for the salvation of non-Christians. We have already given samples of support from the Fourth Gospel of the exclusivist doctrine of

salvation; and just a few lines away from the apparently freeing text now under consideration we read the following: "But to all who did receive him, to those who have yielded him their allegiance, he gave the right to become children of God" (1:12); "For while the law was given through Moses, grace and truth came through Jesus Christ" (1:17). Nevertheless taking John 1-9 in isolation, that is, as "a good idea," large-minded Christians have presented it as a door to salvation for some outside the household of faith.

2. *The secular work of the Holy Spirit.* As for the classical role of the Third Person of the Trinity, the main emphasis has always been upon His work within the institutional church (even in the otherwise liberal United Church of Christ Statement of faith this is the only role affirmed of the Holy Spirit*). But it has been recognized from time to time (and this was true of the predecessor concept of "Wisdom"† in Hellenized Judaism) that the Holy Spirit is loose in the world at large giving a measure of enlightenment for knowledge and empowering for personal and corporate action. Less common has been the delineation of His role as a direct means of salvation; but this unstated inference has enabled Christians to have a hopeful attitude toward the possibility of others' redemption.

---

* "He bestows upon us his Holy Spirit, creating and renewing the Church of Jesus Christ, binding in covenant faithful people of all ages, tongues and races."

† Judaism of antiquity afforded several connotations to the word "wisdom," and while they are not all distinct and inseparable, they correspond roughly to successive strata in the developing Old Testament tradition. Wisdom is compared by Jeremiah (18:18) to the Law or the prophetic word, characterized by the prophet as a sort of skill which underlies the capacity to know. But it is also a form of instruction which leads to the good life (see Ecclus. 8:8), and more important, in late writings it becomes a force similar to the Greek *logos* which "was created before all things" (Ecclus. 1:4). "God understands the way to it, and he knows its place" (Job 28:23).

The direct connection with Holy Spirit doctrine and the Wisdom concept can be seen in the apocryphal *Wisdom of Solomon* and *Ecclesiasticus,* which books both advance the notion that Wisdom is a special grace not possessed by all men, a gift from God which enlightens and raises life into a transcendent dimension. Cf. Ecclus. 24:8 and Wisdom 7:1, 6–7.

3. *"Invincible ignorance."* The Roman Catholic Church developed an apparently expansive concept which had not been hitherto made official by Conciliar or *ex cathedra* Papal decree, but which presumably became official by "case law" in the deposition and excommunication of the illustrious Jesuit, Father Feeney, for his vociferous denial of the concept. This view is that a person who is in invincible ignorance of the claims of the "true Church" is, without his knowing it or even in contradiction to his expressed aversion to it, a member of the true Church and thus may escape damnation. If he has been baptized (through whatever denomination), he could make heaven if he lives "according to his lights" (i.e., as he can best perceive the "natural law").

But this is not as generous as it sounds. All men—even those with the benefit of explicit Church teaching (as Anglican Article IX says, "the infection of nature doth remain, yea in them that are regenerated")—are seen as sinners; and thus few, if any, who have to achieve their salvation by a 100 per cent keeping of their own standards, will make it. The prime example of the extension of the law to those outside the fold is St. Paul's analysis in the second chapter of Romans. But here he uses this uncovenanted illumination as a base of bringing all men (not just Jews) under judgment and of universalizing his point that all men must have their salvation through Jesus Christ. But since the doctrine of invincible ignorance is asserted with a generous purpose, it is to be inferred that less than 100 per cent performance is expected of these *ignorantes*. In any case those not baptized, even those on their best behavior, could aspire to nothing more than "limbo" (the celestial nursery for unbaptized infants)—unless because of a sacrificial death (like, presumably, that of the late James Reeb, the Unitarian minister slain in Selma) "baptism by fire" can be assumed, or a broad view is given (and, happily, is increasingly being given) to the concept of "baptism by desire," namely, that the given person is of the sort who would want to be of the company of the faithful if he knew about the Church and was not too "blocked" from appreciating her claims.

4. *"The Great Assize."* Another "out" which has been suggested from time to time is that apparently offered by the words attributed to Jesus in the passage in Matthew (25:31-46) commonly called "the Great Assize." The Judge assigns to a place "on his right hand" souls who in their earthly pilgrimage served him in good deeds to others, though they were not aware that He was the object of their charity. "I tell you this: anything you did for one of my brothers here, however humble, you did it for me." (Conversely those who denied charity are characterized as having actually denied needed help to Him and "will go away to eternal punishment.") Some who would broaden the possibility of salvation indulge in the assumption that "the righteous" here described who go "into eternal life" (v. 46) are good persons who have not known of Jesus. The purpose of this exegesis is laudable; but it is actually eisegesis. The point of the passage is that the righteous group responded in love to various individuals without direct awareness that in so doing they were in each specific instance serving the Lord, and yet this letter is credited to them. This is fine; but there is no basis of inferring from the passage that the righteous referred to had not heard of Jesus or accepted Him (it is quite evident that the other group, damned to perdition, had)—especially in the light of the "exclusivist" text from Matthew quoted above. And if the two portions of Matthew are to be deemed in conflict, the latter appears to be the normative one.*

* The passage is in some ways a fairly concise expression of Old Testament ethics, and shows similarities to sayings found in apocryphal New Testament books not included in the Canon, e.g., the Gospel to the Nazarenes. Considerable doubt exists as to whether Jesus was speaking of a future messiah in an eschatological sense or of the messianic king of Old Testament hope: the passage most likely represents the interweaving of fragmentary teachings of Jesus with the general outlook of the author of this gospel narrative.

But apart from exegesis and eisegesis, there is a fundamental theological difficulty with this form of the extension of salvation beyond the Christian fold: it would represent salvation by "works" rather than by "grace through faith." We need not go so far as Article XIII of the Articles of Religion which asserts that "Works done before the grace of Christ, and the Inspiration of his Spirit, are not pleasant to God, forasmuch as they spring not of faith in Jesus Christ; neither do they make men meet to receive grace . . . : yea rather, for that they are not done as God hath willed and commanded them to be done, we doubt not but they have the nature of sin." But, as has been pointed out in the section above, no one—Christian or not—can qualify for salvation on the basis of total compliance with the "natural law" or the moral law "according to his lights."

5. *"God's uncovenanted mercies."* The problem just raised above would appear to be solved by another concept which has some measure of support within Christendom, one under which *grace* can be conceived as available to "outsiders." It is this: We who really know of Jesus are bound to God's one appointed way of salvation: faith in Jesus and baptism in His name. But God is not bound by the way He has appointed; His mercies can overflow the "covenant," or, as it has sometimes been put more carefully, we are not in a position to affirm that they cannot. In short, we *know* that Christians can be saved; we do not know that non-Christians cannot.

It so happens that the New Testament writers showed no reticence in filling out the picture. In addition to proclaiming salvation for believers, they plainly decree damnation for the nonbelievers. But if we are to ignore their apparent narrow-mindedness, there are still two other difficulties. First, such an approach leaves definitely beyond the pale those who have had the Gospel preached to them and who have been members of the Church but who honestly on grounds of mind and conscience have chosen another world view. As in the case of the "invincible ignorance" theory, the less the actual ignorance, the less likelihood of salvation "outside the camp." Second, as to those outside all along, *wherever grace is, there is covenant:* both words simply connote relationship with God on a basis of God's acceptance. Whatever religious tradition has enabled a given person to be met in grace, is a way God uses—is God's entree. If the result of the process is salvation for all eternity, what more can the *Christian* hope to gain? We do not proclaim that ours is necessarily an "easy" way. In fact, existentially speaking, there are as many ways as there are Christians, just as the respective configurations of life and the degree of grace at various times would vary among all the non-Christians hopefully receiving "uncovenanted mercies." In short, if this particular theory represents reality, in what sense can the Christian way be declared unique or essential?

Apart from the special difficulties in each of the above theories which would seek to make viable a general approach designed to affirm the uniqueness of Jesus Christ in the universe and yet at the same time leave room for the salvation of some of the vast majority of persons—or possible persons—throughout the universe who are non-Christian, each of these theories fails in one way or another to preserve both of these objectives. Is there an approach which does? Confidence that there is informs the next chapter.

4

Jesus as Man

CONSIDERED AND REJECTED have been four of five possible ways responding to the paradox of the universality/uniqueness of what we see in Jesus: on the left, (a) Jesus as nonexistent or relatively unimportant, or (b) Jesus as a great teacher and example; on the right, (a) Jesus as the absolute and only route to salvation, or (b) the same—with diverse ways of envisioning charitable exceptions. This order of discussion would be arbitrary—indeed quixotic—were it not that the author sees as worthy of consideration another way, one which obviously appears to him to be "the middle way." If there be such, hopefully it is not a "middle way" in the sense of compromise or dilution, but rather a rationale which can express the reality both of the *universality* and of the *uniqueness*. Any such approach would rest on at least the following premises:

1. All reality constitutes a universe. Granted, particularity and separateness of vast numbers of items in the universe is a fact. And granted, particular persons and things do not function in a way which displays perfection of order in the universe. But all things are connected and given a measure of order and of meaning by the fact that they are grounded in their Source, the Ultimate Ground of all being.*

---

* Presupposed here and in the other six premises stated in the text is the dualism characteristic of Western thought (Greek philosophical, Judeo-Christian, and secularist alike) which in theological analysis presupposes a distinction of being between Creator/creature. Oriental thought (religious and philosophical) is characteristically grounded in a monistic (or, perhaps more accurately, a "nondualistic") premise. It may well be (a) that monism is sounder

2. Limiting our consideration now to persons, individual fulfillment consists of knowing and receiving, as far as may be, the meaning of God and relating aright to Him.

3. The way to this fulfillment is the removal, without impairing individuality of personality, of the barriers in us to this relationship.

4. God is universal, and unchanging in His reality and purposes; but His reality as personal is only experienced among men in the particular—in and through particular men, in particular contexts of time and space.

5. Thus it is no contradiction to the consistent presence of God throughout the whole universe and the availability of His meaning and power to all conscious, sentient beings that He becomes manifest in particular men, to greater or lesser degree.

6. There is only one of Him. To whatever degree human beings may participate in the Divine Being, there are no demigods and apart from Him there are no particular divine beings. He can be in and act in and through given human beings to the degree they have freed themselves of barriers between themselves and Him.

(in physics we have already abandoned the matter/energy dualism; and the body/soul dualism is on the way out, due both to the intensifying of the concept of personhood and increasingly greater knowledge of psychosomatic medicine) *and* (b) that the Catholic Faith could be reconceptualized and restated on the basis of a nondualistic view of the universe. The author has begun to think about these two questions and hopes before long more fully to pursue them, not only in the interest of truth but in the interest of the light more such exploration might throw on dialogue between Western and Eastern religions—not only toward the end of greater mutual understanding but toward the achieving of the obvious desideratum of the unity, at the base, of the world's great religions, to the glory of the Ultimate Reality recognized and adored by all of them and for the peace and unity of mankind. Maybe monism is as sound or sounder, or perhaps there is a philosophical truth which is more ultimate than either, and which could embrace whatever truth there is in monism and dualism. Acknowledging these questions, the author is nevertheless at this point only capable of developing an analysis of belief in dualistic terms. But simply to suggest the implications of the acceptance of a nondualistic base for the above premises articulated in the text, the following might be adequate alternative words:

7. The "orthodox" and the unbeliever alike affirm that Jesus was a man. His very being a man means that characteristic of Him, as of other men, was the capacity for freedom—and, as to the most important thing, the freedom to give prior allegiance to, *or* to subordinate, those things which would block an open channel for the manifestation of God in him to the fullest.

Ecce homo! Behold the man.

We have no reliable information about Jesus' infancy, adolescence, or early adulthood. What little there is in the New Testament purporting to deal with this period is in what are apparently late layers of material in two relatively late books of the New Testament anthology—the Gospels of Matthew and Luke. Notable in these narratives are the Virgin Birth stories, which conflict with earlier sections in the two Gospels which set down (from oral sources) two genealogies—inconsistent with each other, incidentally. The "begats" were apparently used forensically to establish what the Jews of the period regarded as an essential requisite of Messiahship, namely, blood lineage from King David. And they lead down to Joseph!* The purpose

---

The last sentence of 1. might read: "Each and every particular thing, while separate from other particular things, is part of the One." (This is *panentheism*— not "pantheism" with which Western religionists have carelessly labeled Oriental thought.)

In 2., in place of "and relating aright to Him" we might say "and recognizing his unity with Him."

In 3., in place of "to this relationship": "to the recognition of our unity with God."

In 6., in place of "many participate in the Divine Being": "can know their identity with the All." And in place of "to the degree they have freed themselves of barriers between themselves and Him": "to the degree that His already-Presence is partially or wholly manifested through their self-awareness."

* Cf. also: (a) the absence of any reference to the Virgin Birth in Mark, the earliest Gospel; (b) a similar silence in the even earlier Epistles of Paul, along with his affirmation that Jesus was "born of a woman under the law"; (c) the absence of the narratives in the Fourth Gospel, whose author in fact allows to stand uncontradicted Philip's reference to Jesus as "of Nazareth, the son of Joseph" (John 1:45, AV).

of the Virgin Birth narratives is understandable. It was fairly common in the Mediterranean world to provide for gods, demigods, and heroes—as the setting for a gem—a miraculous birth as an impressive context; so this seemed appropriate for Jesus too.*

Also it seemed important to the originator or originators of this late tradition to have Jesus literally fulfill what to them seemed an important prophecy from Isaiah, as they read it in the Greek Septuagint: "A virgin shall conceive" (Matt. 1:23 =Isa. 7:14)—though the passage in Hebrew is more honestly rendered (as in the Revised Standard Version) "Behold a young woman shall conceive."

Likewise of the development of the legends about his birth in Bethlehem (to line up the picture with "Bethlehem in the land of Judah, you are far from least in the eyes of the rulers of Judah; for out of you shall come a leader to be the shepherd of my people Israel" [Matt. 2:6=Micah 5:2]), the flight into Egypt (= "I called my son out of Egypt" [Matt. 2:13-15= Hosea 11:1]), and the slaying of the Holy Innocents (= "A voice was heard in Rama, wailing and loud laments; it was Rachel weeping for her children, and refusing all consolation, because they were no more" [Matt. 2:18 = Jer. 31:15]). The process is pretty evident, e.g., from the phrase often used, ". . . in order that the prophecy might be fulfilled."

The story of the visit of Jesus with His parents to the Temple in Jerusalem reveals at most a precocious youth who was already taking religion quite seriously. But certainly plausible—and meaningful—in terms of what follows, is the brief descrip-

---

* But cf. the vehement repudiation by Plutarch (*c.* 50-120 A.D.) of the virgin birth of Numa and the bodily ascension of Romulus (*Numa,* iv, 4; *Romulus,* xxviii, 6-8), which "may, possibly, represent reactions against Christian stories" (Intro. by C.F.D. Moule, *Miracles* [London: Mowbray Ltd., 1965], p. 8), "the vigour of this usually most tolerant man's refutation [suggesting] that he may be arguing against something more immediately relevant" (the late B. S. Mackay, *id.,* p. 110).

tion of the child Jesus' development, which has well served as a
model for wholesome adolescence ever since: "as Jesus grew up
he advanced in wisdom and in favour with God and men"
(Luke 2:52).

We begin with the historical Jesus when we begin with the
earliest Gospel, Mark. In confrontation with the prophet John
the Baptist, Jesus is baptized and apparently at this time (or by
this time) had decided on the rabbinate as a career and, sensing
a calling to fulfill the messianic role, accepted it.* He then went
on "a retreat" and thought out the question as to which of the
four different messianic expectations which were current among
His people, and which were grounded in various prophecies, He
would assume. He rejected three possible roles ("The Tempta-
tions in the Wilderness"): the revolutionary political leader and
imperialist conqueror, the provider of economic need, and the
Oriental fakir. On His return, He made clear that He had
chosen the role of the Suffering Servant, "the Man for others,"
as Dietrich Bonhoeffer characterized him. In His home town,
He read in the synagogue on the Sabbath: "The spirit of the
Lord is upon me because he has anointed me; He has sent to
announce good news to the poor, to proclaim release for prisoners and recovery of sight for the blind; to let the broken
victims go free, to proclaim the year of the Lord's favour
(Luke 4:18-19 = Isa. 61:1-2a). Apparently the significance of
His selection was not lost on the congregants; but He underlined it by the comment, "Today hath this scripture been ful-

---

* Some scholars doubt that Jesus was conscious of (and/or claimed) the
Messianic role the primitive Church attributed to Him, it being suggested that
this is a post-Crucifixion conviction part and parcel of the Resurrection faith
[e.g., Wrede, Loisy, Dibelius, Bultmann; see Werner, *The Formation of Christian Dogma* (London: A. & C. Black Ltd., 1957), pp. 18-21; Bultmann, *Existence and Faith* (London: Hodder & Stoughton Ltd., 1965), pp. 40-43; Mc-
Leman, *Resurrection Then and Now* (London: Hodder & Stoughton Ltd., 1965),
pp. 117-120; Nineham, *The Gospel of St. Mark* (Middlesex: Penguin Books
Ltd., 1963) pp. 32 *et passim*]. But a particular position on this problem is not
essential to the thesis of the present work.

filled in your ears" (Luke 4:21). He was early aware of the cost of fulfilling the role He had chosen: "When the days were well-nigh come that he should be received up, he steadfastly set his face to go to Jerusalem" (Luke 9:51).

A fuller expression of the role He chose is found in the Suffering Servant passages of Deutero-Isaiah, which describe in moving terms the role of the people Israel in the world (or, more precisely, the "faithful remnant," since obviously the cost is high enough to "separate the men from the boys"—a cost so high that in the end it might be narrowed to one person and those sufficiently inspired by Him to "follow in his train"). The relevance of this image to Jesus' choice was obvious enough to early followers of The Way that specific features of it (along with images in Psalm 22) were used by the evangelists in "writing up" Jesus' Passion, with the sincere purpose of identifying their Lord with this greatest of all man $\rightarrow$ God/God $\rightarrow$ man images. Thus it is here set out in full:

So shall he startle many nations; kings shall shut their mouths because of him; for that which has not been told them they shall see, and that which they have not heard they shall understand.

Who has believed what we have heard? And to whom has the arm of the Lord been revealed? For he grew up before him like a young plant, and like a root out of dry ground; he had no form or comeliness that we should look at him, and no beauty that we should desire him. He was despised and rejected by men; a man of sorrows, and acquainted with grief; and as one from whom men hide their faces he was despised, and we esteemed him not.

Surely he has borne our griefs and carried our sorrows; yet we esteemed him stricken, smitten by God, and afflicted. But he was wounded for our transgressions, he was bruised for our iniquities; upon him was the chastisement that made us whole, and with his stripes we are healed. All we like sheep have gone astray; we have turned every one to his own way; and the Lord has laid on him the iniquity of us all.

He was oppressed, and he was afflicted, yet he opened not his mouth; like a lamb that is led to the slaughter, and like a sheep that before its shearers is dumb, so he opened not his mouth. By oppression and judgment he was taken away; and as for his generation, who considered that he was cut off out of the land of the living, stricken for the transgression of my people? And they made his grave with the wicked and with a rich man in his death, although he had done no violence, and there was no deceit in his mouth.

Yet it was the will of the Lord to bruise him; he has put him to grief; when he makes himself an offering for sin, he shall see his offspring, he shall prolong his days; the will of the Lord shall prosper in his hand; he shall see the fruit of the travail of his soul and be satisfied; by his knowledge shall the righteous one, my servant, make many to be accounted righteous; and he shall bear their iniquities. Therefore I will divide him a portion with the great, and he shall divide the spoil with the strong; because he poured out his soul to death, and was numbered with the transgressors; yet he bore the sin of many, and made intercession for the transgressors. (Isa. 52:15, 53:1–12)

We now turn to the principal influences on Jesus' thought, which influences are reflected alike in His teaching and in His actions. Of course, the principal formative factor was, speaking broadly, the Jewish Faith. This seems almost too obvious to say. Yet many Christians have tended to think of Judaism as a totally separate religion, like Hinduism or Shinto, in spite of the fact that the Church early thought that it settled that point in its condemnation of Marcion. (Some Christians are even surprised to learn that Jesus was a Jew!)

But as is true in any major religion, there were various currents of thought, movements, and "parties" in the Judaism of Jesus' day. He was influenced by the Pharisees: He shared their *seriousness* about religion, in marked contrast to the more lax and worldly Sadducees. He stood with them on the side of belief in eternal life for the individual. (The likely reason that the Sadducees had no conviction about life after death is that, being the socially, financially, politically, and ecclesiastically "in-group," they had it so good in this life.) Many things Jesus said sounded like the revolutionary motif of the Zealots. In this regard His words about the Kingdom and His Kingship were threatening to the Roman authors, and the Passion narratives do not give us a record of any attempt on His part to clarify their misunderstanding. But that he was not a Zealot may have been reflected in the rejection of Him by Judas, perhaps disappointed that Jesus was not going to be the "Fidel Castro" that the radical Left were looking for, and in the fact that He curbed the "direct action" impulses of some of His disciples.

The major single influence seems to have been one almost totally suppressed by the writers or final editors of the books of the New Testament and by the early Church Fathers, because it represented an ongoing competitive movement whose tenets and practices were so similar to the followers of The Way that it would appear to cast doubt on the singularity—and as it was later developed, the cosmic uniqueness—of Jesus. I refer to the Essene movement, and particularly—as we continue to learn more about it—the Qumrân Community.*

As is evident from the findings from the Dead Sea caves, the biblical interest of this Community was limited almost entirely to Deuteronomy, Isaiah, and the Psalms, and in such late writings in the Greek *koinē* as the Book of Enoch. The quotations from the Old Testament attributed to Jesus are in good measure confined to these canonical books, and He reflects very strongly the ideas found in Enoch (and to the less vivid forms of them found in late Old Testament writings). For example, like Enoch and the convictions of the Essenes, He believed unqualifiedly in the imminent end of the world, going so far as to declare that

---

* There is uncertainty as to whether, strictly speaking, the Qumrân Community was a part of the Essene sect or a similar but separate movement (see, e.g., Harrison, *The Dead Sea Scrolls* [London: English Universities Press, Ltd., 1961], pp. 95-99, and authorities cited); but for the above discussion it is simpler to follow the broader usage of Josephus in using "Essene" as a general category.

some of His immediate disciples would be alive when the end came. And His frequent use of the "Kingdom of God"/"Kingdom of Heaven" image stems directly from the Essene literature and other books which reflect the introduction into Judaism of the Zoroastrian idea of the conflict of the Kingdom of Light and the Kingdom of Darkness, through the presence of the Persian overlords of Israel in the fifth century B.C. From the Qumrân Community came also what for Christians are the two great sacraments, Baptism "by water and the spirit" and the Eucharist which, as in the case of the Essenes, has added to the blessing of bread and wine as a thanksgiving act—literally "eucharistic"—the image of the Messianic banquet, anticipating on earth the fulfillment which is to come to the saints in light.

To Essene influence we can also trace the ascetic and world-denying notes in Jesus' teaching and in that of the early Church, e.g., as to marriage/celibacy (Matt. 19:12), self-denial, and fasting. A more basic influence is seen in the parallel between Jesus' conception of His role and that of the Teacher of Righteousness, apparently the greatest leader in the history of the Qumrân Community, who also identified with the role of the Suffering Servant, taught along Jesus' lines, and is thought to have been crucified about 50 B.C.

Though more Essene material continues to turn up, at the present time we have through the New Testament books, principally the Synoptic Gospels, considerably more data about Jesus than we have about the Teacher of Righteousness. Certainly whatever Jesus gained in His self-image from the leader, was more fully "spelled out" and acted out. Further, we must not go overboard as to the Essene influence, primarily for two reasons: (a) influence by the other current trends of thought is also evident, and in any case Jesus was a true person, i.e., an individual, and thus contributed His own unique insights to the whole pattern; (b) likewise so did the composite authorship of Matthew and Luke, as well as apparently single authorship of

Mark and John and of the genuinely Pauline epistles and the unknown authors of the later New Testament books. (In the later books, notably the Fourth Gospel, quite evident is a marked Hellenistic influence.)

As rabbi, Jesus' teaching is not—apart from emphasis—unique, nor is there much sign that He intended it to be. His pedagogical methods were such that He was certainly superior to any other rabbi in history in communicating sharply and vividly the theological and ethical teaching of the religion of His people. Marked (though not unique among the rabbis of His time) is His use of parables and His use of dialogue (e.g., answering a question by asking another), now very much back in fashion, reflecting both the Socratic and the rabbinical techniques. He evoked a ready response of understanding and commitment; but, more important than that, He consistently sought to probe beneath the law to the basic matter of motivation and moral purpose and direction. In this He was necessarily iconoclastic, debunking the elaborate absolutizations, particularly of the Pharisees and of the canon lawyers of His day, for the positive purpose of impelling people to act in responsibility and love, from the heart rather than by rote conformity.

The fact that all that He taught was shot through with His conviction about the impending judgment and end of all things earthly gave an immediacy and urgency to His exhortations ("the Kingdom of God is at hand"; "While ye are in the light, walk in the light, for the darkness cometh") and a black-and-white character to the ethical norms ("If one asks thy coat, give him thy cloak also"; "take no thought for the morrow"). This same conviction is reflected also in the early writings of Paul, but not so much in the later ones. (Apparently the holy Apostle had begun to accept the fact that the end was not coming as predicted.) But illustrative is Paul's teaching about marital plans: in paraphrase, "Since it's all over soon anyway, if you are married, stay married; if you are not, don't—unless you really have to: it's better to marry than to burn."

As important as Jesus' teachings were His actions, which were so highly consistent with that teaching. In the Fourth Gospel, intended to display the "supernatural" character of Christ, the miracle narratives are set forth as "signs" of the Divine break-through. They had a "P.R." function rather than being what Søren Kierkegaard calls "the works of love." But in the Synoptics, where Jesus is quoted as saying "there shall be no sign," His work of healing is in response to need by a man of ultimate compassion. Another contrast: in the Fourth Gospel the apparent intention of the miracles is the *evoking* of faith, whereas in the Synoptic Gospels the healing is the *fruit* of faith in God through Jesus. For example, in the second chapter of Mark we read of an arthritic who is burdened with a sense of guilt (or to put it more accurately in terms of modern psycho-somatic medicine, a guilt-ridden person with an arthritic result). Jesus first copes with the spiritual problem, concluding with the assurance "Thy sins be forgiven thee," and then gives the patient confidence in the somatic corollary "Take up thy bed and walk." Through confidence that God accepted him, the weight that burdened his spirit—and his limbs—was lifted.

The popularity of Jesus' teaching and the warmth of His compassionate love demonstrated in fruitful results, attracted more and more people, until He came more and more to bear down on the decisiveness of religious commitment and the surrender of false attachments which was required—at a cost; then His movement began to go downhill, at least as judged by the standards of the compilers—and watchers—of Church statistics.

This was no surprise to Jesus, as we see from His little parable on "counting the cost" (Luke 14:25-33). Even more to the point was His response to the mother who wanted to be sure that her two Apostle-sons were given preferment in the forth-coming organization of the Kingdom: "Can you drink the cup that I am to drink?" (Matt. 20:20–28). It became more and more evident that significance in the coming Kingdom was less like the hope of an honorary degree and more like the opportunity to earn a Purple Heart. Fewer and fewer stuck with Him; and the soundest interpretation of the accounts would indicate that on Calvary His disciples had all made themselves scarce and that He was alone—except for some of His enemies and the Roman functionaries who were about their assigned tasks.

The increasing enmity of the Pharisees and the scribes was obvious. But the crisis seemed to have come with an "outrageous" public assault on the Sadducees, who were the "power structure," in charge of the Temple, and collaborators with the colonialist regime. The entry into Jerusalem carried the suggestion of a kingly role, and that same day He staged single-handedly a surprise "demonstration," in civil disobedience against the law and practice of State and Church, letting the animals and birds out of their cages in the market in the fore-court of the Temple, and interfering with the banking business by upsetting the carefully arranged tables of the money-changers. Now that He had the organized minorities against Him, He could expect no help from the unorganized populace. As in all times, most of them were indifferent but some readily joined the mob, shouting their backing of those who had calculated reasons for getting rid of Him. But at no point did He recant or "bevel off" His teachings. He was convicted by Church and State alike on the grounds of heresy, conduct unbecoming a rabbi (remember that He unembarrassedly ate with prostitutes and little cheats—called "publicans"), civil disobedience, and treason.

Even His most ardent followers seemed to have lost confidence in Him and His movement. But all this changed after His death and Resurrection. The life of no individual ends with his physical death. And as God was fully in Jesus in life here, so was He beyond the grave. And since the completeness of God-in-Christ during His earthly days was due to the absence of barriers in Him to God, so in His resurrected state there were no barriers—from His side—between Himself and others. As for those "on the receiving end," the disciples knew Him so fully and they had become so open to Him, whose character and personality were so transparent, that there was little blockage from their side of the veil to the their being convinced of His personal presence among them, His ongoing life after His death on the Cross.

The credibility of this reality is supported by the fact that His disciples, too, were now filled with a high measure of courage and boldly went out in the streets and proclaimed—in obvious danger of the enmity of those who had ganged up on Jesus—that He whom they thought they had destroyed was alive and that He had been vindicated, and with Him His teachings. Thus began the form of Judaism that is known as The Way, and a type of messianism centered around Jesus, as indeed the Essene messianism had been—and at this time was still—centered around the Teacher of Righteousness. Later at Antioch the followers of Jesus were called "Christians," i.e., Messianists (*Christos* = The Anointed One, the Messiah)—a name literally applicable also to the Qumrân sect.

The movement got off to a good start but was not particularly flourishing until St. Paul sensed a response to this form of Judaism on the part of the Gentile "fellow-travelers" of the synagogues around the Mediterranean in the Jewish Diaspora. These were the "proselytes" or "God-fearers," who found in Judaism with its ethical monotheism a more satisfactory meaning for life than in the official polytheism of the empire or in Mithraism or the other mystery cults but who, not being part of the Hebrew ethnic tradition, were not willing to become Jews to the extent of undergoing circumcision or committing themselves to the dietary regulations. After considerable controversy, the scars of which are evident in the Book of Acts and in the Pauline epistles, the conservative elders in Jerusalem finally came 'round; and the first reported Council of the Church, under the presidency of Jesus' brother, James (the first bishop of Jerusalem, relieved non-Jews of all but three of the traditional Jewish prescriptions (Acts 15:6-29). Thereafter the new movement was well on its way to becoming a world religion, rapidly beginning to win converts beyond the limits of the Gentile fringe of the synagogues.

Thus the role of the Christian movement soon became broader than a role Jesus conceived of as to Himself. For example, in the encounter with the Greek woman (Mark 7:24-30) He declared that He had come to the lost sheep of the House of Israel and used the denigrating word "dogs" of the likes of her. But she answered Him in the same terms and asked that she might partake of the crumbs at the table, and He was then willing to serve as the means of the healing of her daughter. In this apparent conflict between Jesus' role and the later Christian role, neither is inconsistent with the Old Testament, in which are found both contradictory motifs. The high-water mark of the "chosen people" concept in an exclusivist sense is seen in Ezra. At the same time the notion that the Jews were chosen as an instrument to bring truth and salvation to all the Nations is picturesquely and vividly portrayed in the Jonah allegory, where Jonah's reticence to let Gentiles "in on the secret" was forcibly countermanded by God through a shipwreck and the transporting of Jonah in the belly of a whale to a Gentile locale as the forum for his preaching. In any case, the breakthrough of truth and saving power in Jesus was too good to keep quiet about. Indeed there was fulfilled the "Song of Simeon," which in its use in Luke's Gospel is made to refer to Jesus personally (whatever the original poem referred to—probably to the Remnant, the true Israel): "the glory of my people Israel and the light to lighten the Gentiles."

So much for Jesus as man, as a significant religious leader. To sum up, in Him and in the faithful reception of Him we see displayed (both in word and in deed—there being high consistency in Jesus in this regard):

the reality of the universal, personal God, ready and eager to be in relationship with persons, for their fulfillment;

a total claim on life against the minimizing—and thus relieving—detailed codes of conduct;

the central emphasis on accepting love as both the character of God and the motivation and design of man's behavior;

the significance of integrity, courage and sacrifice, grounded in personal eternal life, undisturbed by the worst evils of circumstances or of man's destructive intentions; and

a life, in community, of men who by the sacramental actions of Baptism and Holy Communion publicly and regularly remember the focal point of all this—Jesus' death and Resurrection—and thus continually make present, through this apprehension of reality, which has thus inspired in thousands and millions courage, love, and eternal victory of the same character as Jesus displayed.

If we said no more, we would have affirmed that among all men we have known in human history on this earth—with regard to these most important central things—He is "the most." But because of this very fact, early in the history of the Christian community there was a sense that God Himself is *Actor* in this, there is even more in this than a maximum display of the meaning of human existence by one of God's creatures. So what of the relationship of Jesus to God? Or, to put it in terms which later became common, what of "the Divinity of Christ"?

5

Early Assessments of Jesus

JESUS HIMSELF knew that His role was special, and the early Church was even more conscious of this fact. Those who directly or by inference these days simply say "Jesus = God" find the New Testament puzzling in that nowhere does it appear that Jesus Himself uttered this straightforward declaration. This would have been impossible for at least two reasons:

1. It would have been difficult for Jesus Himself, so thoroughly imbued with Judaism, so to conceive of Himself. The most basic tenet of Judaism—distinctive as among the Mediterranean religions—was monotheism and the utter rejection of the idea of a god in human form.

2. But if it can be imagined that Jesus so conceived of Himself, even with all His courage it would have been unthinkable to utter it: from the moment He would have said it, He would have had *no* chance to do any teaching or make any impression on His fellow Jews. He would have committed the greatest capital crime—blasphemy (they charged Him with that near the end anyway, even without such a blatant assertion on His part, and it was one of the grounds of His conviction and execution).

Had He been God in this simplistic sense and if we had His word for it, His earthly life would be irrelevant to men in any generation: obviously there cannot be expected of finite man what would be attributed to pure God operating among men. This is the very weakness of Greek (and the plagiarized Roman) mythology. From time to time gods came down from Mt. Olympus and worked mighty wonders, but little value of example was found in these things. These are the things gods can do, but men are not gods.

Therefore, in seeking to find form of words for His role and work, Jesus utilized special categories which were part of current Jewish expectations. We find in Daniel, though somewhat vaguely, and in Enoch more explicitly, the image of the Son of Man, and this Jesus used of Himself. It is not clear that He called himself the Son of God, though others did; but this was an ambiguous category, in the sense that it was also used in the plural ("sons of God") in the Old Testament and by Jesus. True, He referred to "my Father," but also to "our Father" and to "your Father." He did not directly call Himself the Messiah, but He spoke of His role in such a way and acted in such a way as to imply the applicability of this title. Jesus obviously viewed Himself as "sent" by God: yet so did the prophets. But unlike the prophets, he was confident that He would come to earth again and serve in a judicial role. In the Pauline epistles, while no greater light is thrown by way of a title, significance is attached by attributing pre-existence to Jesus and by attributing to Him a singular role at the end of things—as Judge, as King of the Kingdom, and as possessing the highest place next to the Father in the Heavenly Court.

In later writings a divine or semidivine status is suggested. In Philippians He is described as being in the *morphē* of God (2:6)—a word difficult to translate with any certainty but which could mean "form," "likeness," "essence," "fashion," or "image." And although all of us are made in the "image of God" (Gen. 1:26-27), He is described as "the express image of his person" (Heb. 1:3, AV). And by now Jesus can be independently worshiped and adored along with the worship of God as such.

By the early second century, the unknown author of the Fourth Gospel goes a good deal further. With the aid of the Logos philosophy then popular in the Hellenistic world, the earthly Jesus is identified with the eternal Word, which was "with God" and "was God" (John 1:1), and "all things were made by him" (1:3). Here words are provided for Jesus to declare His identity with God. For example, "the Father and I are one," "He who has seen me has seen the Father," "before Abraham was, I am" (the latter being the unutterable name of God, "Yahweh"). But in the same Gospel these clear assertions seem to be contradicted. Jesus prays to the Father—in fact at much greater length than in the Synoptic Gospels. This parallels his retort when he was addressed as "good rabbi," "Why do you call me good? No one is good except God alone" (Luke 18:19). And He declared that "the Father is greater than I" (John 14:28). Also "sons of God" appears in the plural (1:12).

The more maximum categories used do not match up very well with the reports of two critical moments of doubt: in the Garden of Gethsemane, "O Father, if it be thy will, grant that this cup be taken from me"; and from the Cross, *"Eloi, eloi lama, sabacthani?"* ("My God, my God, why hast thou forsaken me?"). Nor do they line up with the apparent "adoptionism" of St. Paul's tremendous declaration after the summary of Jesus' *kenosis* ("self-emptying"), "Therefore God raised him to the heights . . ." (Phil. 2:9). But the Johannine texts do display an important checkpoint in the increasing capacity of the spokesmen for the Christian community who were expounding new life conjoined with Christ to find categories which seemed appropriate to His ultimacy in their lives—and by an ontological extension, in the world and in the Universe. And we are well on our way toward the definitions finally arrived at, after much backing and filling, by the episcopate of the Church in the Ecumenical Councils, culminating in the Athanasian Creed—expressing a view of Jesus as God and man to which the Reformers did not readdress themselves and which has remained relatively unchallenged within the Church until the present era.

This work does not purport to be a history of Christian thought or of Christology; but a brief summary will suggest the process. Early was the concept of Adoptionism, i.e., that Jesus was so good that God selected Him for elevation to a Divine role (e.g., in later manuscripts of the Gospels in the narrative of His baptism, the changing of "in whom I am well pleased" to "this day have I begotten thee," in contrast to the Virgin Birth narratives which presuppose adoption at the time of conception or a prior status thereto). The early characteristic effort to image Jesus as divine, but less than God, was promoted by the heresiarch Arian. Jesus was pictured as an eternal subdeity with the Father. Meanwhile the bishops had given Jesus equal place in the new Trinity with the Father and a personified Holy Spirit. So finally, Arianism and an attempted compromise ("semi-Arianism": Jesus is of like substance, *homoiousios*) were rejected, and Jesus was declared to be *homoousios* (of the same substance) with the Father.

There was continuous effort in the discussions of the theologians and in the deliberations of the bishops to keep Jesus "grounded," i.e., truly a man. Rejected early were Docetism, i.e., that Jesus was God "dressed up" as man in order to each men, and later Appolinarianism, which was an oversimplified "Jesus = God."

Later, attention turned to the psyche of One whom the Church was determined to proclaim both as God and as man. The bishops rejected both Nestorianism, which would have presented a schizoid personality (two distinct persons functioning in one human body), and Monophysitism, which affirmed that Jesus was one person, half-God and half-man—which would have denigrated both His Divinity and His humanity.

Finally (and this about marked the end of the process), the Church condemned Monothelitism, which granted the two natures in one person but affirmed that Jesus had only one will—the Divine will. If this latter were true, Jesus would have lacked human freedom of will—and thus would not have been a real man. In this last worthy attempt at clarification, so much time had passed since the Incarnation had been proclaimed— and was now unquestioned by anyone—that no one seemed to notice the inherent contradiction between the condemnation of "one-will-ism" and the assumption that there was a unique embodiment of God in Jesus at His conception. If Jesus were God from the beginning—right from His infancy—up to the time He made with His human will, like anyone else, a decision about His vocation, wherein was His human freedom? If Jesus were truly man (and the Church has insisted that this is the case) with freedom of will, at the time of the call to the rabbinate (which presumably was coupled with the call to Messiahship), He could have said, "Things are going very well for carpenters in Nazareth; this is no time to become a rabbi. And as for Messiahship, the times are so troubled that is a risky business." It is not irreverent to suggest this, since obviously He did not make this choice; but the glory of the choice He did make rests upon His freedom to make it. His then following the calling of God is relevant to our responsibilities in crucial moments of decision in our lives, precisely because He freely made the decision as man. But suppose He had made the "practical" choice and settled down in Nazareth, married, raised a family, and died in His own bed. This would not be an unworthy thing for a pious Jew to do. But if He had from the beginning been God incarnate, it is difficult to conceive how at this point of decision He could then have been *un*incarnated.

An additional but perhaps more transient difficulty is the fact that in the development of the history of thought, the ontological categories used by the bishops in the fourth and fifth centuries to define Jesus are no longer a part of the equipment of men today—either of intellectuals or of the common man. "Substance," used in a metaphysical sense, is even more meaningless that it is now in the science of physics; "nature" in the "two-natures-in-One-person" sense is not meaningful to the modern mind; and "person" as used in the three-persons-in-One-substance" of the Trinitarian formulation has radically changed its meaning from "mask" to that of distinctive personality.

Therefore we should endeavor to rethink and to restate the answer to the old question "What think ye of Christ?" in a way which preserves three things: (1) the fact of Jesus' full humanity and individuality as a human being, (2) the fact that in the experience of the Christian community Jesus is sensed as belonging to the ultimate dimension of reality, and (3) the fact that God Himself, as the Ultimate Ground of all being, is unchanging and universal in His reality and ways, and though He is revealed through the teaching and lives of many, many human beings—and very conspicuously in some, and though each of these manifestations is special, nevertheless *God* is not acting "specially" at any time.

For quite awhile many have been taking a "new look" at the question, quite a few in lectures and sermons and some in books. What will be attempted here is by no means entirely original and will have merit only in that it is addressed to the right problem in terms of viable contemporary thought forms, and thus may contribute a measure of clarity and intelligibility to the whole ongoing current effort toward an understandable, coherent, and credible Christology.

6

God in Christ

THERE ARE three requisites to a coherent and relevant image of Jesus:

1. It would have to take account of the obvious fact of His centrality in the community known as the Christian Church. It is its *raison d'être* and the basic explanation for its amazing first flush of growth in the Western world, for its indomitable continuity in the face of persecution without and weakness and corruption within—being by far the corporate institution of longest standing in history (as the Calvinist Beza said, "The Church is an anvil which has worn out many a hammer"), and for its present life throughout most of the earth.

2. It would have to be consistent with a sound view of God, particularly in regard to the point (numbered 3) at the close of the last chapter: what we see of reality in the operation of God in the image of Jesus must not be arbitrary or "special" on God's part, no matter how "special" we may regard Jesus.

3. It would have to keep Jesus "grounded" on earth: nothing must compromise the fact of His full and complete manhood; otherwise His life, death, and Resurrection would have no relevance for us who, at least in this period of our eternal existence, are definitely earth-bound.

And along with these three things, a fourth, almost too obvious to state: whatever we come up with should be in accord with the truth, insofar as we are able to perceive it.

God is presented paradoxically in the Judeo-Christian tradition: (a) He is "human" in making special decisions, changing

His mind, getting angry, forgiving, readjusting the normal course of astronomy, meteorology, and biology to accomplish a specific, localized objective or to help any particular cause which appeals to Him, etc.; (b) He is unchangeable, both in His purposes and in the uniformity of His ever-availability in relation to every person and thing, with "no variableness neither shadow of turning" (Jas. 1:17).

Passages of Scripture and notions of Church Fathers and other theologians, confessions of faith, etc., supportive of the other view to the contrary, (b) is the far more plausible view and is presupposed in what follows. But in opting for this concept of God, it is important to stress that He is not—as some philosophers who have been in this general school of thought say or imply—passive and immovable. He is active, He is moving—"on the move."

More especially, His relationship to us is dynamic. He is like the steam under the lid, pressing against it to the bursting point. This pressure of God against the barriers in us which block us—to greater or lesser degree—from participating in Him, corresponds to the conventional category of "prevenient grace."

His involvement in an individual life is not something added to the natural ideal; it is not something "supernatural." The condition of a person blocked against God is not natural; it could be called "subnatural." Without that freedom from the barriers of idolatry of persons, things, and fixities of historical pattern, without full freedom as a person, one is not really a whole man. Jesus as man was, as far as we can see from the data about Him, virtually totally free from these barriers; thus God could fully operate in Him and through Him. Jesus was so fully a man; hence what we see in Him is God at His fullest. This is not supernatural; Jesus is, among those we have had the opportunity of knowing anything about, a man most Himself and thus God is seen as most Himself—most natural.

Perhaps the qualifying adverb used above—"virtually"—

should be explained. It would be less than honest to recognize that there are a number of passages in the Synoptic Gospels which might suggest a qualification in our generally taken-for-granted conviction about the absolute perfection of Jesus. The claims of candor would require that we not gloss them over in any case; but we need not fear to face them, since, as we shall see, they do not disparage the pattern arrived at. For example:

(a) His initial "brushing off" of the Gentile woman hoping for the healing of her daughter, and His humiliating response to her, although it all worked out in the end, would seem to represent rather unchristian behavior. Alternative explanations are possible. The purpose of Jesus and/or of the evangelists who provide the narrative may not have been directed toward a lesson in pastoral care, but rather a lesson in missiology. Mission begins where one is with one's own immediate associates, with the plan that this company shall carry the message beyond these limits. A good policy—supported elsewhere in Scripture: "Ye shall be my witnesses both in Jerusalem and in all Judaea and in Samaria and unto the uttermost parts of the earth" (Acts 1:8). (It has also been suggested that He was "testing her faith"; but this is rather unconvincing. We do not consciously deliver hurts to people's sensitivities for even that good an end!)

(b) In dealing with the case of a couple of multiple schizophrenics in the locale of the Gadarenes, He is reported to have driven the many demons out of the patients into a herd of swine, who, as an immediate result, rushed down a cliff and drowned in the Sea of Galilee. Jesus' gifts as a psychic healer are evident from the Gospels, and there is no particular reason to doubt the authenticity of the claimed recovery of men in even so complex a schizoid condition. But it is evident that the interests of the owner of the herd, which might well have represented his whole life's savings, were given no particular consideration (and had there been an Israel S.P.C.A., there might have been a protest about the fate of the animals). There is, for example, no indication that at that point a collection was taken up to

provide compensation. And entirely understandable is the closing line in the pericope: "Thereupon the whole town came out
to meet Jesus; and when they saw him they begged him to leave
the district and go" (Matt. 8:34). A "way out" on this narrative is of course that, without doubting the healing, we could
presume that the Evangelist embroidered the story re the new
housing for the demons.*

(c) If we assume that the "exclusivist salvation" notion from
the Fourth Gospel (purportedly supported by words from
Jesus) did not really represent the true Jesus (but rather an
early—and persistent—unfortunate development in the Christian Church), we yet have to deal with what one of the com-
mentators has called a "johannine bolt from the blue" which
appears in two of the Synoptic Gospels: "Everything is entrusted to me by my Father; and no one knows the Father but
the Son and those to whom the Son may choose to reveal him"
(Matt. 11:27 = Luke 10:22).

Already referred to has been the contradiction in Judaism,
reflected in the books of the Old Testament, between a universal
forum for salvation and an ethnic club. While the conversation
with the Gentile woman might seem to indicate that Jesus had
opted for the latter, this is not at all clear; and certainly, as we
have seen, early organized Christianity followed the first alternative. But in the above words attributed to Jesus there would
seem to be support for the other kind of exclusivist salvation
which has been the prevalent motif in organized Christianity. As
we indicated in Chapter 4, it is bad enough for the Church to
have held this view so long and so widely, without having it
attributable to the Church's Lord. Since this text is *sui generis,*
so far as the three relatively reliable accounts of Jesus' teaching
goes, one can indulge with plausibility in the hope that the

* Cf. the view of the matter taken by the third-century Neoplatonic critic of
Christianity, Porphyry (in *Adv. Christ.,* fr. 49), as summarized by Dodds, *Pagan
and Christian in an Age of Anxiety* (Cambridge: Cambridge University Press,
1965), p. 125, n. 4: ". . . probably fictitious, but if genuine then morally dis-
creditable."

words are not authentic, perhaps an interpolation at the hand of someone familiar with the Johannine presentation.

But in any case, few are the possible reservations one could have as to the perfection of motivation and reaction in Jesus. (Thank goodness the Church Fathers decided to exclude the Gospel of Peter from the Canon, in which the little Jesus is seen magically destroying His playmates with whom He had had a quarrel, albeit He thereafter miraculously brought them back to life). So we see clearly Jesus is what St. Paul sums up in Philippians 2: a man beholden to no one and to nothing, free of values which most men then and ever since have tended to absolutize—house and home, success, financial means, popularity, the drive to win, and self-preservation. He also sat loose to a fixed schedule, responding ad hoc to needs which He encountered as He went along, dominated at all points by truth, integrity, and, most important of all, concerned and accepting love. As part of the same parcel, He both sought to communicate tellingly the meaning and applications of this kind of loving, and He *did* that which He talked about, in His response to existential situations, focally in the Great Response in His passion and death. Indeed, with no loss of His individual, distinctive (and obviously magnificent) personality, He "emptied himself" and took the form of a servant, and was obedient to the overall Claim—even unto death, to the death of the Cross. Under the one Claim He was thus free of all other claims, as the image in His parable of the centurion who could exercise his responsibilities without fear or threat because above him was the authority—and claim—of Caesar. Paul Tillich throws light on this kind of freedom with the help of three fairly complex words: Those who seek *autonomy* ("The serpent said to Eve, Ye shall be as gods,") fall into *heteronomy* (bondage to persons and things; cf. the Prodigal Son); but if they change and their lives reflect *theonomy,* they have the stability and steadfastness which gives them freedom from all else—a freedom well expressed in Archbishop Cranmer's translation of an early medieval prayer: "whose service is perfect freedom."* This is in fact a mistranslation (but an inspired one); the original is arresting also: *"cuius servire est regnare"* ("whom to serve is to reign").

Returning now to the role of God, obviously here is a human avenue whom God—the whole God (not one of three Persons) could fully fill. And at the same time, speaking of Jesus as man, we can see that with etymological accuracy, He was fulfilled. St. Paul summed it up in two illuminating texts: "God was in Christ reconciling the world to himself" (2 Cor. 5:19); and "For it is in Christ that the complete being of the Godhead dwells embodied" (Col. 2:9). Even if there were a few blocking facets (e.g., if we were to take at face value the apparent negatives discussed above), there is here displayed God—and more than anyone needs of a grasp upon what God is like, especially in relation to men (the important thing for all men to know and enter into), and in Jesus as man there is all—and more—than anyone needs of a model as to what man is to be like. And this is what every man is called to be like, as is made clear by the fact the familiar passage in Philippians 2, in its context, is not really primarily about Jesus but about us. It begins: "Let this mind be in you, which was also in Christ Jesus: who . . ." (vv. 5-6, AV).

The task of the Christian then is *Imitatio Christi,* and if he has chosen this as The Way for his progress toward fulfillment, he will have more than ample to do and be, and, existentially speaking, in his life Jesus Christ is unique. Is this affirmation relativistic? Whether it is or not, certainly a Christian must affirm *this* in any case; otherwise there is no existential reality to the commitment. But can one declare, in addition to this necessary evangelical affirmation, an objective, universal uniqueness? To this question we next turn.

---

* Book of Common Prayer, p. 17.

7

Jesus Christ as Unique

"LET THIS MIND be in you, which was also in Christ Jesus . . ." expresses well the fact that *potentially* every man is *alter Christus*. Indeed, this is the calling of every man. We are not called to *Imitatio Christi* in the sense of a plagiarism of His precise words and deeds. An old-fashioned method of teaching rhetoric or oratory was to assign the students an essay or speech by one of the "greats," e.g., Cicero or Edmund Burke, and, taking a modern contemporary topic, to write it over, duplicating sentence by sentence, phrase by phrase. Some people think that is the way we are to follow Christ; hence the all too common sermon topic: WHAT WOULD CHRIST DO TODAY? Obviously, the contexts of decision-making today are markedly different from those in which Jesus operated, and also Jesus' distinct human personality was "peculiar" in the original sense of that word, as indeed every individual's configuration of personality is peculiar—and this is good. Hence, both what the person's gifts and responses are and what they are to be brought to bear on, differ immeasurably from the contexts and responses we see mirrored in the Synoptic Gospels. Thus wisely, St. Paul did not say "Be like Jesus"; he said, "Let this mind [i.e., spirit, attitude, stance, freedom, integrity, etc.] be in you, which was also in Christ Jesus."

The possibility of actualization of this potentiality in each of us is not a matter of law or of theory; it can be—and for many has been—verified in experience. Many of us have found ourselves involved in confrontations in which at least "for the duration" we have managed to empty ourselves, care nothing for reputation, and act as servants—obedient to the overall Claim as it seems to apply in the context. And we have experienced in such a period the operation in us, and through us, of truth, accepting love and new life. The difference between these examples of *kenosis* and the day-by-day, week-by-week, and month-by-month life of Jesus is not a difference of kind but a difference of degree—degree in two senses: (a) the extent to which in such episodes we were really freed of self-centeredness and other "blocks," and (b) the proportionate amount of our whole span of life in which true *kenosis* obtained.

The very putting of the question in this way will evoke (and it has evoked!) the pejorative label "relativistic." Is it? In the end, no. First, let us clarify the connection of words which will be used in answering the question:

$$\frac{\text{Ontological} = \text{Qualitative} = \text{Kind}}{\text{Existential} = \text{Quantitative} = \text{Degree}}$$

We can ask the question in two ways. In fact because of the dualistic thinking which is ingrained in Western minds (whether dualism or monism is in fact more sound philosophically),* we inevitably will look at the matter from two perspectives: in any assessment of Jesus, God and man are involved. Thinking of God—in general or with particular reference to His involvement in Jesus—we are of course affirming the Absolute, and here, both in general and with reference to Jesus, we are affirming a difference from all else. This is ontological, qualitative, a difference of kind. When we are thinking of men—either in general or with particular reference to Jesus the man (since there are no demigods or other divine beings beside the Divine Being)—we should think existentially, quantitatively, assessing the difference of degree. But even in this, in regard to Jesus, the *outcome* is not relativistic. It is relativistic as to the process, but not

* See pp. 45-47, n.

necessarily as to the answer. The grading of an examination in calculus, particularly for professors who grade "on the curve," is relativistic in method but not in result. One student out of a class of thirty may receive the only "A," others receiving B's, C's, D's, and F's; and that student is, without any equivocation in the use of the word, unique.

This process is unfamiliar to most Christians. And this is true of the clergy as well. In few seminaries is careful objective study given to other world religions and their central figures or to the life, character, and import of "singletons" like Socrates. All I remember from my theological education about other world religions are some "snappy" forensic answers which presumably could demolish their significance in a single blow. For example, "The Oriental religions are world-denying; the religions of the Book are world-affirming." Or, "They're pantheistic." Or (as to Zoroastrianism), it's "dualistic" (as if Christianity weren't!). And yet we presume to declare that we *know* that Jesus is the "best," "unique,"—"the only." This rather consistent posture of Christianity (now, happily, being modified somewhat by some Churches in the "line" used in missionary areas) gives us one clue as to why (along with the rising nationalistic spirit in many of these newly-freed nations) there is strong resistance and hostility even to our presence there on mission. It is unadulterated arrogance. *Not* because we have come to the conclusion we have about Jesus, but because we have done so without considering alternatives—alternatives which have nourished their religious life and culture.

One reason (and there are others) why many parents are opposed to their children's "going steady" at too young an age is that their conviction that a given member of their peer group of the opposite sex is "the one and only" is a premature conclusion based on too narrow an empirical base. Likewise, how do we have the gall to say—not for home consumption to the "in group," which is more forgivable, but to our secularist culture here, or to the cultures elsewhere otherwise religiously-oriented —that Jesus is "unique" or "the only route to salvation" without any—or with trivial—knowledge of alternatives?

Since the "famous last words" of Socrates were set forth at some length earlier in the book, let us start with him. Even the casual reader, with only a lay knowledge of the Passion narratives and the Gospels, would not have missed the almost direct parallels between most of these statements attributed to Socrates and the words of Jesus. Tempting is the speculation that through the nexus of Alexandria, the center of both Hellenistic culture and Jewish culture after the fall of both Greece and Israel, Greek *koinē* being the lingua franca of both cultures, the authors and editors of the Gospels may well have been familiar with Plato's *Apology* and *Crito* (as Paul was familiar with Greek philosophers [e.g., Acts 17:22–35]) and that Socrates' reported words may have influenced the account of the Passion. But this hypothesis is by no means necessary. The response of Socrates and Jesus to somewhat similar "binds" are—once one has read them—the ones to be expected of two men of utter integrity and freedom from the "false gods." But there are two important differences, one relating to content, the other to corporate contexts:

1. Both were persecuted for truth's sake. Both were engaged in the iconoclastic task of debunking the premature finalities of the best—not the worst—men of their day (this is why Jesus was more contentious with the Pharisees than with any other group: they were about the most religiously earnest ones). But as important to Jesus as truth, was love. And there is nothing we have in the record as to Socrates, that this was at the center of his teaching or witness. True, his desire that other men know the truth and that they be freed from what Percy Dearmer has called "the familiar lies,"* particularly as he asked and received

---

* *The* [Episcopal] *Hymnal 1940*, Hymn 299.

no compensation for his tutelage, was the acting out of *agapē,* and evidence of this kind of love was also seen in his forgiveness of his enemies and his affirming to his judges that he loved them all—though he pronounced a measure of doom upon them (which Jesus didn't hesitate to do either). But teaching about love as an essential ingredient—along with truth and integrity— for human wholeness, is lacking. And to the degree that Socrates' freedom from false attachments permitted the Ultimate Ground of Being to work in him and through him, we do not see displayed here what we see obviously displayed in Jesus, namely, that God is Love and that the whole man is grounded in Love. This is meant as no criticism of Socrates—would that more Christians who have talked so much about love throughout the centuries, had had an equal respect for truth and openness to truth, and expressed the proper amount of agnosticism which saves men from idolatrous finalization of contemporarily acceptable concepts and words, codes of behavior, cultic practices, and forms of ecclesiastical polity. We need more Socratic "gadflys" in and around the Church (we have canonized a few, but usually long after they were safely dead!).

But the particular configuration of his personality and perhaps the context of his time did not bring through him Love, as a dimension of the Divine Being, to light. And it did in Jesus.

2. While any famous (usually in his own times, = notorious) figure is in "apostolic succession," with predecessor spirits, and in turn has successors to carry on his influence—and this is certainly the case of Socrates—yet this great teacher was essentially a "loner" as compared with Jesus. Jesus was a member of a corporate body, founded many centuries before (archetypically by Abraham)—a people visibly united in covenant with God, one which continued visibly (in both the Old and the New Israel) without a break in the centuries after His death. In tying ourselves to Jesus, we tie ourselves to more than Him. We tie ourselves to a whole texture of thought, relationship, and

action; we become part of this visible society which nurtures us as indeed we nurture it, and through it, hopefully the world. There are no Socratic Churches (and unfortunately few socratic ones); but there are Judeo-Christian synagogues and Churches. One need not deify the Church as institution to recognize that the Church in its visible continuity is an impressive manifestation of ongoing, corporate life and witness, providing within the body widely variant expressions and "break-throughs" of the central meanings of God and man thus carried from person to person, from generation to generation. In Jesus and His larger family, before and after His time, we have a setting for the Gem. It is thus not surprising that (though *vox populi, vox dei* is not in itself a reliable norm) an enormously larger number of human beings have been followers of Jesus than have been followers (indeed if there are any, in any usual sense of the word) of Socrates.

The second distinction just made does not apply in the comparison between Jesus and Buddha. He too is set in the center of a large ongoing group-tradition. Hinduism is to Buddhism as Judaism is to Christianity: there is a continuous history. There is another analogy: Buddhism went over better with "the Gentiles" than with the home-folks. It has had little place (until recently) in India where the Gautama lived and taught, but it is the principal religion of peoples farther East, just as Christianity became the principal religion of the nations to the West, with few adherents at any time in Jesus' homeland. Thus the text, "a prophet is without honor in his own country" (John 4:43). Just as in the case of the Christian, one who identifies with Buddha (except more recently in the case of most of the WASP* Zen Buddhists) usually identifies with the Buddhist religious community and shares in and contributes to the contagion of faith.

* "White Anglo-Saxon Protestants."

Here again there is an important difference—centered on the
matter of love. But to evaluate it we must make a distinction
between the two main forms of Buddhism, the *Theravāda* and
the *Mahāyāna*. These correspond roughly to Catholicism and
Protestantism within Christianity, the former claiming to be in
direct succession with original Buddhism, the latter claiming to
have restored the real meaning of original Buddhism. The point
can be illustrated by the difference in attitude on one question;
is it moral for a Buddhist to seek to complete "his own salvation" and achieve full detachment from "the changes and
chances of this mortal life" without regard to the exercise of
agapē toward others in the form of tarrying to help bring them
along the way? To this important question the normative answer for Theravāda Buddhism is yes, and the normative for the
Mahayana is no. For the former group, in a sense, each man is
on his own. The latter maintain an attitude that is reminiscent
of a motif seen in the New Testament by some Christian theologians that for none of us will salvation be complete without
salvation for all. But for the adherents of both, salvation (to
continue to use our Western word) consists in Enlightenment
(i.e., in the case of Socrates, truth; but in the case of Buddhism,
the truth about *who one is*—God-consciousness. Just as in the
case of Socrates, concern that others appropriate truth is in fact
an expression of *agapē*—though neither Socrates nor the Buddhists precisely possess this concept). But *agapē* in the prior
sense of positively moving out to meet the needs of persons in
their existential situation is not central in either form of Buddhism. Classical Buddhist writings (and particularly of the
Mahayana denomination) conceive of *mettā* (roughly trans-
latable as compassion) as a desirable ethical flowering of the
"Enlightened" life, whereas in Christianity it is seen as part of
the essential and primary message, and something to be gotten
to right away ("if any man will do His will, he shall know of the
doctrine" [John 7:17, AV]). Here honesty—about both Christianity

and Buddhism in practice—compels us to say that we are not here comparing the actual behavior of given Christians and given Buddhists. Many Buddhists are loving indeed, and many Christians are not. But here we are comparing images eligible for religious focus, not comparing persons. Deeper than that, we are comparing what is revealed as to the nature of God: through Jesus and Christianity it is more evidently seen that God is Love.

The difference in the expected outgoingness of love is seen rather simply in the difference between the Oriental "do not do unto others what you would not have them do unto you" and Jesus' "Do unto others what you would have them do unto you." In practice persons, individually and corporately, more often than not fall far below even the first norm (enabling Dr. Dagobert D. Runes in his recent important little book *The Jew and the Cross** to assert that positive "dialogue" is not necessary and to plead that we just stop the hurting. And, further, many a Buddhist (and in some of the literature this is explicitly commended) has acted positively in his neighbor's behalf. But there is a significant difference in the negative and the positive form of this ethical expectation. Thus, on the basis of the matter of the centrality of love, both as an urgent claim upon religious persons and as integral to God, one can quite plausibly choose Christianity and its central figure, Jesus.

Therefore, we can affirm of Him, in a genuine sense, uniqueness, and, to use a contemporary colloquialism, regard Him as "the most." He is truly *our Lord*.

---

* New York: Philosophical Library, 1965, p. 35, *et passim*.

8

The Treasure

"I AM THE WAY, the Truth, and the Life," we read in the Fourth
Gospel (14:6). While, as we have already seen, the negative
conclusion of the sentence ("No one cometh to the Father but
by me") won't do, the opening clause beautifully reflects the
experience of the early Christian community of the role of Jesus
in their lives. To sum up, in Him they saw what a man is to be;
and since Jesus was Himself fully this, they saw showing
through Him the fullness of God as Truth (which in good measure we can see also through Socrates and Buddha as "free and
open" men) and, certainly as important, as Love.

But here is a paradox. In seeing God as Truth, i.e., the Ultimate, we see the Claim on our lives as total. The *Sh'ma Yis-
rael** is not a "law which God decided to impose" (as Jews and
Christians have supposed God imposed a whole lot of laws).
Rather, it is a necessary corollary of the very fact that He is,
that we are persons with freedom—and hence responsible for
our choices. And since there is only One of Him, the Claim is
total; every aspect of our lives is "under judgment."

God as Truth simply *is* this. But, as seen in Jesus, God as
Love, when we recognize that we are not perfect specimens of
the *Sh'ma,* accepts us as we are, enabling us to accept ourselves, and with a motivation of thanksgiving to become more
acceptable ("justified by grace through faith unto good works"

---

* "Hear, O Israel, the Lord thy God is one Lord, and thou shalt love the
Lord thy God with thy whole heart, thy whole mind, thy whole soul and thy
whole strength."

[Eph. 2:8, av]). Are these images of God, as seen in Jesus (not only in His teaching, but in His doing) as *totally requiring* and *totally accepting,* consistent with one another? Here is where we sense in Jesus—especially in His Cross—a third aspect of the meaning of God. The paradox is seen as resolved in the Event with no diminution of either God's righteousness or of His Love. This we call the Atonement. Christian thinkers have developed half a dozen or more theories or "doctrines" of the Atonement; but the Councils of the Church have officially affirmed no one of them. Just as we can affirm the Resurrection without settling its precise mode, and accept the Real Presence in the Eucharist likewise, so with the Atonement. And each of these doctrines, the result of dedicated thought (and we should give *"A* for effort": we are to serve God with our whole mind), is suggestive of meaning, but no one of these theories is in itself satisfactory and a couple of them simply won't do. For example, the "substitutionary" doctrine which became the basis of the introduction to the Prayer of Consecration in the Book of Common Prayer,* implicitly attributes to God a morality we deplore in His creatures: the requirement of a "payoff," a "pound of flesh." And "the contest with the devil" theory, which is celebrated in the familiar Easter hymn "The strife is o'er, the battle won," is mythological to the point of being fanciful. But the composite image of the manifestation of righteousness and love in the painful passion and death and the Resurrection victory, though not logically diagrammable, as a *Gestalt* affirms in action the reality of what God is in relation to man—as expecting the most and accepting the least. And through faith in God through this central manifestation, and aided by the example of others inside and outside of the Christian fold, men have, in greater or lesser degree, fulfilled their high calling in righteous-

---

* ". . . who made there (by this one oblation of himself once offered) a full, perfect, and sufficient sacrifice, oblation, and satisfaction, for the sins of the whole world . . ." (p. 80).

ness in the confidence of acceptance by God for the life here and hereafter.

The Resurrection of our Lord presents no special theological question. The basic question is, does the individual personality survive into eternity? If the answer is yes, then of course this is true of Jesus. If the answer is no, then Jesus as man did not survive either (of course there is no question for a theist as to the eternal life of the One whose full Being broke through in Jesus).

The conflating of these two subjects is not a modern notion: St. Paul did it nineteen hundred years ago: ". . . Christ was raised from the dead. . . . But you may ask, how are the dead raised? In what kind of body? . . . There are heavenly bodies and earthly bodies. . . . So it is with the resurrection of the dead. What is sown in the earth as a perishable thing is raised imperishable. . . . Sown as an animal body, it is raised as a spiritual body" (1 Cor. 15:12, 35, 40, 42, 44).

So a word on the universal matter: personal eternal life. If we say yes, it will not be on a basis of proof; it will be a matter of faith. Faith can be blind, or it can be based on what seems to be the more plausible of alternatives. As to the Resurrection of Jesus this would mean that faith (1) that personal life is eternal and (2) that the Apostles experienced the real presence of the resurrected Jesus. Each of these convictions is more plausible than its alternative.

1. As to the first conviction, there are two bases of plausibility: (a) The person is more than his physical mechanism: even without conscious decision, it is always, cell by cell, dying and experiencing resurrection. And it can be consciously changed by operation and mechanical implementation—and by weight-losing and weight-gaining. The tensions of physical bodily life need not be seen as the tensions of the person. (b) For every basic and universal human desire, there is a corresponding reality. This is obviously true of hunger, thirst, and the urge for

sexual fulfillment. Therefore, more plausible than the alternative is the assumption that this is true likewise of the well-nigh universal yearning for personal ongoingness.

2. As to the second conviction (the disciples' apprehension of our Lord's continuing life after death), there are likewise two bases: (a) The experience was corporate and multiple.* Hence quite implausible is the assumption of individual personal hallucination. (b) The public testimony of the disciples to the experience was at a cost and, in the temper of the time to personal *dis*advantage as far as reputation and safety goes. Hence fairly implausible is the assumption of group fraud.

While the two convictions are separable, in fact the second backs up the first. Faith in our Lord's Resurrection has always supplied existential support for the Christian's hope of eternal life.

What of the quality of life after death? The images of heaven and hell remind us that survival through the grave does not itself necessarily mean a happy outcome. In this life a person is "grounded" in God precisely to the degree that he is able to be open to God's ever-present reality. The more a person is "blocked" from this fulfillment, the more applicable to his situation is the word "hell"; the more a person is open to this fulfillment, the more relevant is the word "heaven." This view of the matter presupposes human freedom. Now, if there is personal and individual life beyond death it is the life of free persons, persons capable of increasing or diminishing their degree of openness to the working of the same God who is experienced during the earthly stay. To affirm that the fate of each individual is eternally fixed as of the moment of death is to assume either (a) that the God related to after death is a different Deity than

---

* And, it must be granted, inconsistent. See McLeman, *op. cit.,* cc. 12-18. This evident fact can be used as an answer to the position that the accounts were corporately contrived; but it does raise problems, e.g., the implications which arise from the Jerusalem/Galilee inconsistency.

the One operative now and/or (b) that beyond death an individual no longer has freedom—which means that what survives is less than a person: it would be an object, a thing.

Were it to be supposed that at death individuals are forever classified into one of two absolute categories—a state of complete bliss or a state of total torment, there is an inherent contradiction. Were the latter a fact, the former could not be. Presumably to qualify for heaven the candidates must have displayed some capacity for *agapē*. So how could such loving persons be content in a heaven from which God has permanently excluded others with no chance for personal change or hope of ever receiving personal fulfillment? If these in heaven were really loving persons, their consciences would compel them, at the least, to stage a demonstration before the throne of the Most High or, more than that, to organize a "rescue party" to seek to save the lost. And, failing all that, they should want to identify with the suffering ones—in other words, go to hell themselves, at any cost to themselves. This would be in accord with the image of sacrificial love for men on this earth so fully displayed in the life, passion, and Cross of our Lord; such a mission is the greatest glory attributed to Buddha; we should certainly not expect less of those eligible for heaven.

Therefore it is more plausible to believe that personal continuity means the continuity of the freedom to be increasingly (or decreasingly) open to the Ground of one's being, to become men (or less) whole.

"But we have this treasure in earthen vessels.* As we have

---

* Critics have noted (e.g., the Rev. Jerome F. Politzer, s.t.m., a priest of the author's diocese, in *Christianity Today,* Sept., 1965) that in this text St. Paul by "earthen vessels" means the ministers of the Gospel, not the concepts and words used to express the Gospel, as the phrase is used in *A Time for Christian Candor* and in this sequel. But the words are used in both books, by relevant analogy, as a useful "earthen vessel" to express a vital philosophical distinction; and, further, directly applicable to the religious point both of St. Paul and of the author is the closing clause of the text: see the concluding paragraph of both books.

seen, the vessels are various shapes and sizes, of varying degrees of utility and inutility. *What is this treasure?* The brief answer, and one which ultimately is adequate, is: God. No one or nothing else is final or ultimate ("I am the Lord thy God and thou shalt have no other gods beside me"). *But:* God, as He has been able to be revealed, through the openness of men to Him —and uniquely in the full openness of Jesus—necessarily entails certain corollaries. These are not special realities or special laws, but are integral to God Himself as we have known Him. Hence, the following answer to the question which forms the title of this volume is a bit longer:

> *God, the Ultimate Ground of all being,*
>> personal and thus valuing persons,
>> Claimant over all,
>> actively ready to break through into the life of every man, as meaning,
>>> accepting love and
>>> new life now and always,
>> Who was able, through the freedom, openness and wholeness of Jesus, to break through fully in Him,
>>> Whose life, death, and Resurrection we recall and celebrate in community,
>>> through which we identify with Him and
>>> seek to free ourselves of barriers to full relation with the Reality Who is already there,
>> we thus being means through whom others to whom we relate as persons, may experience
>>> meaning,
>>> accepting love and
>>> new life now and always,
>> that more and more men may be more and more free, open, and whole, like Jesus our Lord.

This is the Treasure: it is the ALL THAT which serves as the title of the opening chapter. "That's all there is to it," i.e., all that is absolute. Do we need more finalities, more absolutes? It depends upon the depth of our faith in *the* Absolute. The answer is no, if we can join in mind and heart with this affirmation of St. Paul: "Such trust have we through Christ to God-ward: not that we are sufficient of ourselves to think anything as of ourselves; but our sufficiency is of God, who also hath made us able ministers of the New Testament; not of the letter, but of the spirit: for the letter killeth, but the spirit giveth life" (2 Cor. 3:4-6, av).

The answer is more belief, fewer beliefs. Apart from the historical and philosophical differences between the Treasure and the vessels, even more profoundly significant is the religious difference. We can claim credit—or take the blame—for the various vessels, but not for the Treasure; and the recognition of this fact is basic to true religion: "But we have this treasure in earthen vessels, *that the excellency of the power may be of God, and not of us.*"

Index

[*Omitted from the Index are references to frequently mentioned topics such as God and Christology, and as to Jesus reference is made only to specific aspects of His life.*]

Scriptural References

Format by Ronald Farber
Set in Linotype Granjon
Composed, printed and bound by The Haddon Craftsmen, Inc.
HARPER & ROW, PUBLISHERS, INCORPORATED